Ernie Rann

Growing Up in the Oil Patch

D1738696

Growing Up in the *Oil Patch*

John Schmidt

Canadian Cataloguing in Publication Data

Schmidt, John, 1923-
   Growing up in the oil patch

Includes bibliographical references.
ISBN 0-920474-57-8

1. Martin, Frosty. 2. Phillips, Tiny.
3. Petroleum industry and trade — Canada — History.
4. Gas industry — Canada — History. 5. Petroleum
workers — Canada — Biography. I. Title.

HD9574.C32S3 1989   338.2'728'0924   C89-095071-7

Photo on page i —
(L to R) Frosty Martin, Fat Gloyd, Eugene Coste, Garrett Green
and Tiny Phillips.

Photo on page ii —
A.P. (Tiny) Phillips
Glenbow Archives, Calgary, Alberta.

Composition: Video Text Inc.
Design: Steve Eby
Editorial Consultant: Elizabeth Lancaster

Printed and bound in Canada by Hignell Printing
Limited

Contents

These were the days

Martin & Phillips took a contract to drill
a well for The Black Diamond Oil Co
the first contract & well up Sharp Creek

George E Buck was president of the
Co. and promotor (some promotor) he took
the well over at 1800 ft. formed his own
Co. the Janie Earl Drilling Co. bought
some tools and started up in a couple
of weeks pumping tools up and down in the
hole they got pay-sand. but not in the
hole or well. George shipped it in by
the Can. solted the hole made a fortune
and wound up in jail. Turner Valley
first production and stock sold.

Black Diamond Oil 1913.

This was first production from T.V. sold
by the bottle to suckers for stock

Chapter 1

It All Started in Pennsylvania

In 1958, Calgary was a real cow town and the drinking laws were not yet civilized. The big-spending oil crowd, around town as the result of the opening of the big Leduc field, were driven crazy because no-one could take a female companion into a beer parlour. There were no bars serving liquor. If a woman wanted to help drink Alberta into solvency, she had to go into a beer parlour marked "Ladies."

There was one exception to these archaic laws and that was the Elks Club. A couple could drink together in public in the Elks ladies' lounge, providing both were suitably dressed at all material times.

I thought I had arrived at the top of Cow Town's social heap one afternoon when a Hussar rancher, Jack Murray, invited me to join him and his wife at the Elks Club. Murray had a well-stuffed wallet that day, as he had just sold one of the biggest steers ever marketed at the Calgary Stock Yards: a 2,400-pound grassfed Hereford-cross.

As a farm writer, I had been on hand to record the historic event for *The Calgary Herald*, had asked the right questions in a businesslike way; hence Murray's invitation.

He fitted in well with the easy informality of a small foothills city, where everyone knew everyone else and business was carried on on a handshake basis. He deemed it a privilege to introduce a greenhorn from the East, to some of the players in the agriculture field and the oil patch. Both were rapidly adding wealth to the city's surging economy. After a couple of Hudson's Bay Jamaica rums, he said:

"You ought to write a book about some of the fellows who did the bull work, to get this province under way from its inception, in 1915. There's one of them sitting in this very room. Hey, Tiny, come on over here. I have a pencil pusher here, who can whip that book of yours into shape for you."

From a table along the far wall came a wiry, bespectacled little wisp of a man who sat down at the table and, in a mild, tremulous voice began spinning yarns about his experiences as a driller and mechanic, in the oil patch all over the continent. He had worked in them all. He brought in thousands of wells spewing thousands of barrels of oil and wells whooshing millions of cubic feet of natural gas per day — wells which made a lot of people rich, as the result of his know-how about pounding bits with old cable tool rigs, hundreds of feet into the proper oil- and gas-bearing strata.

This was A.P. Phillips, whom everybody knew as Tiny because of his small stature. In a few minutes the air was filled with a freshet of high-energy yarns, tales and myths about the commercial oil industry which sprang up near Tiny's home town in Pennsylvania, only a decade and a half before his birth.

He knew many of the players in the new industry and knew how they operated. He was proud of his own accomplishments in the oil patch, yet he talked more about his "pardner," Frosty Martin, who had died three years previously in Long Beach, Calif., at age 82. Tiny was still mourning the loss.

"Yes, we saw it all from almost Day One in the United States," he said proudly. "We were both born in 1873."

That put Tiny's age at 85 and here he was spry and chirpy, downing drink for drink with the upscale crowd at the Elks Club.

He was born at Oil City, which was near the scene of the famous Drake Well. It was the first big commercial well in the U.S. Being so close to this historic event, its impact had never dawned on them. Although they later participated in drilling similar wells in their time, they were just workaday assignments in a new age of technology.

"Frosty was a terrific mechanic, inventor and entrepreneur who made and lost two fortunes but died rich. But he always came to see me. He never forgot me. I was always his pardner," said Tiny.

"I have it all written down in a scribbler at home, how we drilled all those wildcat wells which opened new fields. You come on over and I'll show you my scribbler about the oil patch."

Using the back of a couple of coasters on the table to make drawings, he launched into a detailed description of the inventions made by Frosty to allow drillers to sink wells faster.

A few days later I was sitting in Tiny's comfortable living room in his small, modest home on 12th Ave. S.W. Yes, he was right, he and Frosty had seen it all. The scribbler proved to be an informal oil patch history textbook covering half a century. The first sentence in the scribbler read:

"Albert Parker Phillips was born Jan. 13, 1873, in Oil City, Venango County, Pennsylvania."

Such a bald statement is of little moment. But to an oil historian there is plenty of significance, realizing the added fact that his father was an oil driller before him, right on the ground floor of the commercial industry.

In 1859, Seneca Oil Company despatched Edwin L. Drake to have that first commercial well drilled at Titusville, only 20 miles from Oil City. Drake's qualifications in an industry with no benchmarks: He was a young railroad conductor with crippling arthritis. His usefulness to Seneca — after being high-pressured into buying $200 worth of company stock — was, he could travel free on his pass.

Although drillers in Oil Springs, Ontario, dispute Drake's claim he drilled the first commercial well in the world, it was production in the Oil Creek Valley, that showed an oil-hungry American industrial complex it could depend upon oil drillers for assured future supplies. The drillers played a significant part in maintaining America's world industrial leadership right into the space age.

Phillips' accident of birth in the heart of the area that cradled the infant industry, allowed him to grow with it. His own career parelleled oil's startling expansion and, at the proper time, both were Alberta-bound. As he noted in his scribbler:

"I was brought up around an oil rig. An oil rig was my playground. My dad taught me how to fire a rig boiler at an early age. In fact, I could tell how many pounds of steam were on a boiler's steam gauge before I learned to tell the time."

The most unlikely persons were engaged in the oil industry: sawmillers, lawyers, prize fighters, brakemen, professors, water well drillers and actors. Phillips' father, Samuel Anthony, could be considered in the "unlikely persons" class when he left his job at the Pennsylvania Tack Works in Norristown, to go to Titusville about 1869. He had apprenticed as a blacksmith. He had heard there was plenty of work for men of his ability, in the oil fields forging drilling tools.

When Tiny came along things had not tamed down from the wild, unruly and hectic times that marked the transformation of a quiet rural area. The gambling, lawlessness, loose women and two-fisted drinking, which were the hallmark of most early American mining camps had now become part of the oil town but had not yet been submerged by a more respectable society with the family as its centre.

However, by this time men who had previously worked seven days a week, now had their pockets full and were content with only six days of labour for themselves and their employees. Machine and

A.P. Phillips at age seven, is pictured third from right in the front row. This classroom photograph was taken in Norristown, Pennsylvania.

Albert Parker (Tiny) Phillips. Photo: Lanes Studio, Calgary, Alberta, circa late 1920's.

Away from the Findlay Oil Field, A.P. Phillips played guitar in local theatrical productions.

blacksmith shops which had been busy 24 hours a day, were down to a steady 12-hour day.

At first there was work for hundreds of coopers making oak barrels that held 300 pounds of oil. The cooperage business was pinched off, when somebody got the bright idea of mounting two wooden tanks on a railway flatcar. Flatcars were later discarded, when somebody else got the idea for the industry's first successful pipeline.

Blacksmiths were the kingpins in the years prior to S.A. Phillips' arrival. "Uncle Billy" Smith, the man whom Drake hired to drill his well, was a blacksmith. Up to that time oil had been collected from seepage along the creek banks — and yielded about six gallons a day. But the Seneca company wanted a faster way of bringing more oil to the surface. Smith, with experience in drilling salt wells at Tarentum, Pa., was hired at $2.50 a day.

The ubiquitous scribbler recounts Tiny had visited bewhiskered Uncle Billy, when he had retired to his farm to hear him tell stories about drilling the Drake well. After he had begun the job, he had been offered a blacksmithing job at Franklin for $4 a day. Although

Tiny Phillips (foreground). Bearded man is Uncle Billy Smith, other individual unidentified. Moberly, Missouri, circa 1900.

This photo taken in 1900, shows A.P. Tiny Phillips (left), unidentified man (centre) and Uncle Billy Smith (right).

Drill rig at Moberly, Missouri, 1901.

he was tempted to take it because he liked blacksmithing better than drilling, he decided to stay with Drake and see the job through.

Had he not stayed the first well might have been abandoned half-way to completion.

The drilling was blessed by a lucky break. It was drilled directly over a crevice in some rocks. A fair flow was struck at 69½ feet. Had it been drilled in another location oil would not have been struck at that shallow depth, because there was no similar formation anywhere else in the area.

Titusville got more press coverage than the California gold rush 10 years previously. This was possible because the Drake well was brought in within travelling distance of 31 million people. Nobody had to trek 2,000 miles; it was right there at the back door for them to visit.

When Tiny was a tad, the telephone hadn't even been invented and oil refineries were just springing up. The only refineries available to handle the immense flow of oil were modified whale-oil refineries. Oil was refined chiefly for kerosene for lamps. There was to be no demand for gasoline for another 40 years.

But the industry built 23 refineries in Titusville by the time Tiny was born.

Whale oil was the chief lubricant of the day, but the whales were at the point of depletion. They would have become extinct had not the new oil source come along as an alternative.

Titusville was there before the oil boom and there afterward. It didn't suffer the fate of places like Pithole City whose population was zero one day, 15,000 three months later and zero 500 days after that. During those 500 days it was the "sin city" of the U.S. That was because it had every other kind of civic service and business but no law and order. Only one other city had a worse reputation. That was Petroleum City, Pa., before a vigilante committee was organized of necessity. The Phillips' scribbler has a note:

"Old-timers used to tell me with faintly nostalgic smiles, about the parade of 100 whores who rode sidesaddle on a tour of the main streets, as a preview of the night's business."

Slick practices, scams and thefts were part of the scene. Apocryphal or not, one of the favorite stories of Phillips is how one of the finest farms in Ontario was bought by a young Canadian, who got rich quick on the outskirts of Pithole City, merely by taking a rest by a pile of wood beside the road. He was approached by a man on horseback who mistook him for the owner and offered him $4,500, for the 300-cord wood pile.

Before he could demur, the man thrust $4,500 in cash into his hand and disappeared down the road. He was back in a few minutes with wagons and teams and began hauling away the wood.

There was hell to pay when the proper owner showed up and found half his wood pile gone. A search was made of the bars for the young Canadian but he was well on the way toward Lake Ontario.

It was poetic justice that Pithole City was able to make a valuable contribution to redeem itself: the first successful oil pipeline. This innovation came about because of the transportation monopoly held by teamsters. Anyone who visualizes that today's Teamsters Union is composed of hard-bitten, arrogant men almost law unto themselves, should have been in Tiny Phillips' territory to observe the anarchy of their unorganized predecessors who drove horses. There were thousands of them hauling three to seven barrels of oil in their wagons.

They started out charging $1 a barrel, but later began gouging producers for as much as $5 for the haul to the railroad. They were law unto themselves and when producers tried to haul oil in their own rigs, the teamsters hit back with violence.

Nobody lifted a finger against them until Samuel Van Syckel came along. Up to that time, the teamsters' lobby was so strong the Pennsylvania Legislature refused to pass laws granting charters to pipeline companies. However, the producers became desperate and finally forced the politicians to grant a charter to construct a pipeline, from Pithole City to a railhead five miles distant.

Van Syckel was hired by a transportation company to build the line in 1865. He came in with a bunch of toughs determined to beat the teamsters at their own game. They put together a line of two-inch iron pipe and tested the joints, before burying it in a two-inch trench. The downfall of previous lines was the joints leaked; welding hadn't been heard of yet.

Besides tight joints a new principle of pumping oil had been devised, to make the new line more efficient. A rotary booster pump was installed halfway along to maintain pressure.

When the Teamsters discovered Van Syckel had started pumping 800 gallons a day for $1 a barrel, they were furious. They attacked and engaged in mayhem.

The end came when one of Van Syckel's men was shot and killed. Van Syckel found the teamster boss in a bar in Titusville and beat him to a pulp with his fists. The teamsters collapsed and pipelines became an established means of oil transportation.

This innovation brought to an end the murder of some of the horses. Up to the time pipelines were installed, every gallon of oil from the wells had to be hauled in barrles on drays to railhead or water through oil, grease, mud, clay, ooze, muck, filth, stench, grime and dirt three feet deep in most places.

Contributing largely to the mud and mire of the roads and streets were 12,000 horses and 12,000 mules. Although the need for horses diminished after the building of the Erie Railroad and the coming of pipelines in 1865, there were still thousands of horses and teamsters engaged in short hauls. During the height of oil hauling, it was not uncommon to see a solid line of teams a mile or more long heading north out of the valley to the railroad. These processions went on slowly from dawn to dusk seven days a week. One man, to win a bet, counted 2,000 teams crossing the bridge on the main road out of Titusville in one day.

A further note in the Phillips scribbler about the treatment of horses in the pre-Humane Society days:

It was said that mud and crude oil, one of the stickiest and most corrosive mixtures ever brewed, ate the hair right off the poor brutes leaving them raw, sore and bleeding. Many had not a hair below their necks. The oil on the roads kept the mud from drying in summer and from freezing in winter.

Mudholes were four to eight feet deep. They were kept constantly liquid by barrels spilled from overturned wagons. If wagons upset, the barrels were abandoned because it was not worth the trouble of trying to reload them.

Much of the oil was shipped out by the pond freshet method. During low water on Oil Creek barges wouldn't float. But agreements were made with sawmill and grist mill owners, to hold water in their dams for a week or so and at a certain time release it, creating a small flood that would float the barges. But they had to be dragged back and this was done by horses pulling them walking along the creek bank or creek bed.

This operation was plain murder. More horses were killed on Oil Creek than in the notorious Deadhorse Gulch, through the White Pass, in the Yukon Gold Rush 40 years later.

On this backhaul job, horses were up to their bellies in cold water in winter. Slush and ice shaved off their hair. Large chunks of ice hung on their tails.

The whips of the unmerciful teamsters took their toll of tufts of hair and even the lives of the poor brutes. It was cheaper to rawhide a horse or mule to death, than give it kind treatment. The teamsters were in waist-length rubber boots, ready to jump out of the barges to whip a horse to death if it balked at a difficult stretch of the river.

A single trip realized a handsome profit and new horseflesh was easy and cheap to buy.

Father Samuel Anthony moved the family around several times, while applying his trade as a blacksmith in the oil field. He had married Anna Liza Disel, a farmer's daughter from Titusville, in 1870. They moved to Oil city in 1873, where Tiny was born. The next year he formed a partnership with Anna Liza's three brothers to drill oil wells. Later he went back to Norristown and formed a partnership with his two step-brothers to drill artesian wells.

This partnership was short-lived as, when Tiny was 10, his father died leaving the family destitute. Tiny went to live with his uncle, an optometrist. At age 12 he began serving an apprenticeship with his uncle. But at 14, he knew that prosaic trade wasn't for him. He wanted to go for the excitement of oil drilling. He took off to join Anna Liza's brother, Ami, to go into the drilling trade. However, Ami had moved to Findlay, Ohio, where a new oil and gas field had been brought in during 1884. It was promoted as "the largest gas belt of any now known in the world."

Later the city public utility commission was the envy of the nation, by giving gas away to attract industry. Its slogan was: "Women Split No Wood In Findlay."

Chapter 2

Apprenticeship in Findlay, Ohio

Gas wells had been brought in during the oil rush on Oil Creek but gas was treated as an unwanted byproduct. Most was flared off as there was no other use for it. A well at Murryville, Pa., blowing out 34 million cubic feet a day, burned out of control for 1½ years. This well proved production was large enough and constant enough, that users could depend on the supply for commercial use to replace manufactured gas.

Curiously, there was public resistance to switching to natural gas, as people had developed a healthy fear of it after several had been injured in explosions.

When Tiny arrived at Findlay the big excitement there was the Oesterlen gas well, which had touched off the oil and gas rush in that state. The drillers for the well were Brownmyer and Martin of Bradford, Pa. The Martin end of the team was Milton Martin.

Milton and his brother, James Gelot Martin, were both drillers, sometimes working together, sometimes independently or teamed with others. Frosty was the son of James and nothing could keep him in the old Taylor School after age 16 to stop him from becoming a driller.

The Martin brothers got into oil drilling in 1861 — earlier than the Phillips. They lived a rough, hard life, almost nomadic in character, following a schedule of moving around but part of a pioneering society that somehow stuck together.

Ticksford, Grease City, Crown Pulley, Glycerine Hollow, Karns City, Butler, Red Rock and Bradford were all Pennsylvania boom towns at which the Martins were employed during the first dozen frenetic years of the Keystone State's new-found industry.

In 1873, the best home James Martin could find available for his wife, Hattie Jackson, was a shack near a well-drilling site in Grease

City field. Frosty first saw the light of day in that shack Sept. 6. By his own accounting, he tried to drown out the noise from the hillside stripper wells with his squalling.

Grease City is not on the map today. Thus it was that an "obit" writer in the *Long Beach Independent* upgraded his humble birthplace to "Greece City."

Another Grease City native was Maud Jamison. Neither child knew of the existence of the other, until 19 years later when they met at a ball game in Findlay. Maud was a young teacher in Findlay College — and she was going out with a speed-crazy young man, Barney Oldfield.

Barney and Frosty were members of the Findlay Bicycle Club, which had a quarter-mile dirt track with turns banked 10 feet high. Oldfield always beat Martin — but he was left out of the competition for Maud's hand the day she met Frosty. They married that year. Oldfield continued racing and later became one of the stars at the Indianapolis Speedway 500-mile races.

The first quarter-century of the Martin marriage was one of constant moving and travel under varying conditions of poverty and affluence. There were periods of loneliness for Maud while Frosty was away in the field. There were several trips around the wourld.

In their later days of lavish living in Long Beach, California, the days of living in tents in the field were forgotten. Their 57 years of marriage were exciting and full of devotion and ended with Maud's death a year before that of Frosty.

Their first child was John Walter, born in Medicine Hat, Alta., in 1912. He acquired the nickname of Spud almost from birth when the proud father, with his off-beat sense of humour, told some of the boys on the rig: "I spudded in — and look what I got." (Spudding in was related to the necessity of digging a hole before setting up a cable tool rig.) They raised as a son, Harold J. Blythe, the infant son of a cousin who died. He, too, acquired from Frosty the nickname of Baldy and it stuck with him better than his Christian name, until he died in 1963, after following the drilling trade in his younger days.

A note in the Phillips' scribbler on nicknames: "Frosty was bigger and huskier than me. His blond hair and light complexion earned him his name, Frosty. In the rough-and-tumble drilling fraternity, I would start fights and Frosty would step in and take over.

"No matter how far we drifted apart we never lost contact with each other. Sometimes he would be in California and I was in Pennsylvania. It made no difference: he would look me up or I would look him up. We were pardners and we helped each other finish many jobs."

By 1884, the Martin brothers could see the end of oil drilling in the Pennsylvania fields. When the chance came to move to Findlay, to drill the Oesterlen gas well they seized it. The success in drilling this well resulted in them being given contracts for a series of good producers. Findlay became the Mecca for the biggest and best pool of drillers in the United States, for more than a quarter of a century.

Although only 11 when he moved to Findlay, Frosty had already begun an apprenticeship with his father. In his time, youngsters were initiated into family enterprises at an early age and it didn't hurt them a damn bit. Parents didn't believe in child labour; it was mostly that, to keep the kids from getting underfoot in the house. Mother often suggested the boys "go with Dad today." As soon as many could walk, they proudly "went with Dad" and Dad was just as proud to take the son along. Oil was a dinner table topic and by the time he was old enough to take on household chores, night and morning young Frosty had a good indoctrination into the drilling business.

When he was eight, his father and uncle had acquired three little old strippers, (wells in the last stages of efficient production), near their home. It became his job to "do chores" around the wells. He was up with the family at daylight to stir up the banked coal fire under the boiler, get up steam and pump off the wells. Then it was time to go to school.

Returning in the afternoon, there was more work to do. On Saturday he had another job — helping Dad dig up enough coal to fire the boilers for the coming week.

And did he ever get heartily sick of choring around these wells? No, he couldn't get enough of hanging around drill sites and picking up all the knowledge available. School palled upon him. There was no excitement, compared to watching a well come in or watching the men torpedo a well with nitroglycerine.

Going to school was boring beside the excitement generated by the Martin family in the big Findlay field. Frosty became an expert at knowing which days to play hookey to see some big action like the Karg gas well come in. It burned for four months before being controlled. People could read newspapers by its glare at night 10 miles away. It heat was so intense the ice melted on the river, flowers came out in bloom, trees into leaf and grass grew profusely.

Nobody cared that 1.5 billion cubic feet of gas were wasted. Wastage of gas, (nobody ever thought of shutting off a gas light and gas street

lights burned all day), and a lynching, (a good old American institution), were the subject of a page in the Phillips' scribbler:

"It happened when a North Baltimore man went beserk and shot
his wife and started after his daughters. They escaped. He was jailed.

"To show how mob psychology works, a bunch of oil men who
were normally good fellows, were incited to march to the town cop
and demand he unlock the jail. When he refused, they obtained a
big drill bit and broke down the door.

"They grabbed the accused, put a rope around his neck and led
him up the main street to a bridge. They threw the rope over the
top girder but when they pulled on it, the girder cut it and it broke.

"They knotted the break and took him down the street to the
first hydro pole. One fellow climbed the pole and put the rope over
a crossarm and the mob started to pull the prisoner up again.

Some of the inflamed mob out for blood — anybody's blood
— started to shoot at him. The fellow who climbed the pole had to
climb up to the top to keep from getting shot, too. He would have
been killed without a qualm had he not taken this evasive action.

"The wretch on the end of the rope met a horrible death — and
I remembered the savagery for a long time."

Tiny was out of school and working in the Findlay field as a tool
dresser and driller at 14. But Frosty had to put in time with the books
until age 16. Since both were in the same trade, they met somewhere
in the field about this time.

Like all drillers, it was their ambition to buy a string of tools and
go to work for themselves.

Frosty achieved this goal first — by the time he was 20 — and
undertook contracts in various Ohio fields. He managed to do this
by limiting his whisky drinking. The scribbler explained:

A tour of duty, (they pronounced it "tower"), was 12 hours. In
the other 12 hours there was usually no place to go. Most of the men
spent their pay as soon as they made it. There was always the next
day's wages.

The bulk of the pay packet went for booze. After the first shot,
the original idea of saving to buy a rig or lease and become a millionaire
usually evaporated. But Frosty transcended the temptations to which
his fellows succumbed. He was determined to become independent.

It was this burning ambition that overcame the gruelling physical
demands, of working on a cable tool rig. Also, he had recently become
a married man.

Few outsiders could understand the psychology of oilfield crews
and their capacity for whisky, which was bottomless. They could

always depend on working hard the next tour to sweat it out of them. A wag posted his schedule in the bunkshack:

11 p.m. — Get up
11 - 11:30 p.m. — Sober up
11:30 - midnight — Eat
Midnight - noon — Work like hell
Noon - 3 p.m. — Get drunk
3 - 3:30 p.m. — Fight
3:30 p.m. — Go to bed

In this atmosphere, there was an air of recklessness, some shooting, fights, a few murders, (oil tanks hid bodies for years), and general hellery. And not a few suicides.

There were good and bad employers, but one Tiny always remembered was Honest Jim Kirkbride of Rollersville, Ohio. On the third well Tiny drilled in that field for Kirkbride, the crew lost control of a gusher spewing out 20,000 barrels a day 150 feet into the air. It took two days and the efforts of two other crews to close it off.

As the crews walked into the wellhead to install a casing nipple and two eight-inch flow lines, choking, stinking crude oil covered them from head to foot ruining all their clothes. Kirkbride gave the three crews an unforgetable Christmas present when he had his brother, Ed, come down from Toledo and measure every man for a new suit.

As in every other industry, the oil industry goes in boom-and-bust cycles, despite what Keynesian economists would have the public believe. It was during a bust cycle that Tiny Phillips and Frosty Martin found themselves on a Chicago-bound passenger train in 1897. In the suburb of Harvey, Ill., their curiosity was aroused by a large sign, "Well Tools," above the yard of the F.C. Austin Manufacturing Company.

When they left Chicago both had new jobs: Frosty was hired as a salesman and designer of water well tools and Tiny was hired in the warehouse. The idea was, Frosty would sell a string of tools and Tiny would go into the field to erect a drill rig, with the help of experienced drillers he would hire in Findlay. They would string up the tools and start drilling for the buyer.

Tiny figure the Austin company had given him his first big start in life, with some security. It was therefore on May 1, 1902, Tiny married Zulah May Hagerman, a telephone operator in Findlay. She was also a friend of Maud Martin. The honeymoon was partly business and partly sight-seeing.

The business was to superintend the drilling of a wildcat gas well, in the semi-desert mountainous area near Woodside, Utah, for a syndicate which bought the rig from the Austin company. The newlyweds had never heard of the place, but Zulah said she was willing to go and live in a shack in the field, after a trip to Salt Lake City.

It was with a sense of adventure and thrill and possibly a little trepidation that the young couple boarded the train. They were a handsome pair, she dressed in the long floor-length dress of the period with white blouse and huge flowered hat, and he in the plug hat and typical high white collar of men's fashions at the turn of the century.

At Denver, they boarded the narrow-gauge Denver and Rio Grande Western Railroad for the trip to Woodside. This was one of the last narrow-gauge railways in the U.S. It was built that way to enable the engineers to round the sharp curves and make the steep climbs

Tiny Phillips helped bring in the J.W. Kirkbride well in 1895, at Rollersville, Ohio.

through mountain ranges and river canyons. From the windows of the toy coach, they observed some of the most spectacular mountain scenery and also some of the most desolate stretches of terrain in the West.

The train crew were friendly, as are all railway men with newlyweds and joshed them a great deal about that new job Tiny was going to at Woodside. The scribbler noted:

"They asked us if we knew anyone at Woodside. We said no, but we weren't worrying because the syndicate would look after us. We didn't catch the knowing winks the two men exchanged.

"After lunch, the brakeman asked if we wanted our trunks put off. I assured him we wanted to have all our belongings with us. I couldn't understand why he laughed.

"The train left the small town of Green River and the country became more wilder and desolate. In a while, they stopped at a small station. We got off — and could only see one house. The conductor

This camp at Green River, Utah, was built out of railway ties in 1902. Tiny and Zulah Phillips arrived here as honeymooners.

assured us that this was the whole town of Woodside. He laughed uproariously at our discomfiture.

"We at last tumbled to the fact the crew had been kidding us all along. We got back on the train with sheepish looks and a little frightened and crestfallen. We continued on to Desert Siding, which was a mileboard with the name on it, nothing else. The crew was helpful and suggested we go on to Helper, a small railroad town near the famous Moffatt Tunnel."

It did have a hotel and they took a room there to await events. A company man came in from Salt Lake City and told Tiny to make his plans to set up camp, back there in the desert. Tiny ordered the materials, then while they were being shipped in, he and Zulah boarded the train to Salt Lake City, to enjoy the sights and listen to the organ in the big Mormon Tabernacle.

Tiny's boss came out from Chicago and told them he was glad they had enjoyed their honeymoon, but that the drilling location out in the desert with temperatures that went as high as 110 degrees, was no place for a woman and suggested Mrs. Phillips return to Findlay, "for the time being."

The "time being," turned out to be a year before the newlyweds saw each other again. But they accepted this as a way of life in the drilling game. There were no complaints. The wife of a driller never knew when he went away on a job, when he would return.

The reason for his enforced stay at Woodside, was the poor and irregular supply situation. Often the crew had to shut down for days awaiting delivery of casing, pipe, tools or parts.

So while Zulah sat it out in Findlay alone, Tiny and his crew spent some of their spare time exploring the Green River Canyon, whose scenery is almost as spectacular as the Colorado River's famous Grand Canyon. They saw many rare and awesome sights.

After all the effort and time spent on the well, it turned out to be a water well. It was half a century before drillers came along with more powerful equipment that could make more than pinprick perforations in the ground, as Tiny's rig did, (1,000 feet) — and they discovered trillions of feet of gas.

Tiny arrived back in Findlay the next May, vowing to Zulah never to be out on a job so long again.

To make good his pledge, he bought a small store.

Chapter 3

Transporting Nitro to Pelee Island

*O*ne day in the summer of 1904, a man walked into the store. He had a drilling proposition on Pelee Island. Tiny could hardly wait to get home to tell Zulah about this exciting new venture, that would make them all rich.

She signed resignedly and said "Yes, but this time I'll go with you — and stay, too."

And so began an adventure that was to take him to Canada for life; and make him a member of the Elks Club in Calgary.

The man who came to visit him, represented a syndicate of New York financiers formed to drill on some oil leases they owned on Pelee Island, 14 miles offshore from the town of Leamington, Ontario in Lake Erie. It is the southernmost point in Canada. Sandusky, Ohio, is across the lake.

Tiny sent for Frosty, who was in California. They agreed to take on the contract late in the summer. For eight years before that, Frosty had gone wildcatting in Texas, Mexico and California.

It can be imagined, that Zulah was sitting close to the conference table. She was taking no chances that Tiny would go off somewhere for another year and leave her alone in Findlay. Thus when they left for the job, both she and Maud Martin were along. This was despite the fact they'd be living in rough bunkshacks on the isolated island.

Oil had previously been discovered on the island. It was being barreled and shipped to Sandusky in the steamer, Lincoln. Lincoln and another steamer, Excelsior, supplied the islanders — mostly fishermen, with provisions.

When Tiny and Frost arrived with two tool dressers, they found the first job they were expected to do, was clean out two wells already drilled with Canadian pole tools. Pole tools were an ancient type of rig, consisting of 20-foot hickory lengths screwed together like pump rods. The rods hung on a rope strung through a pulley at the top of a 40-foot derrick. One end of the rope was attached to a springed bull wheel, to keep it taut.

The outfit was driven by a steam engine with an upright boiler. The drill bit was not attached to the end of the pole rigidly, because the pounding action of the pole up and down at 25 to 30 times a minute, would cause excessive breakage. The rod was actuated by a walking beam which, in turn, was actuated by the steam engine.

When it became necessary to pull the pole out of the hole, a winch was used. Since there was no reverse on the engine, it was necessary to attach a 100-pound weight to the rope, to bring it back down to the derrick floor. This weight was called a cow sucker — but nobody knew why.

The pair decided to improve the drilling efficiency by buying a No. 5 Star drilling rig. They had no money, but Frosty went across the lake and talked the National Supply Company of Toledo, Ohio, into selling a rig on a "$1 down and $1 when you can catch us" proposition. It was said to be one of the first of its type in the Ontario fields.

There was plenty of everything on the island but money. The residents were nearly all Canadian fishermen, friendly folk who used pound nets and sail boats. There was always fresh fish for Zulah and Maud to cook.

To make money, Frosty hit upon a profitable little scheme. He would buy a carload of casing from the National Supply Company and sell it to the syndicate at a profit. The casing was brought over on the steamers and hauled by wagon to the well by his fishermen friends.

Another of his little money-making schemes did not find favour among his new-found friends, who were unwitting accomplices. The drillers were paying an inflated $3.50 per quart in Leamington, for nitroglycerine, for shooting the wells in the limestone strata. Frosty hit upon the idea of buying the nitro in Toledo for half the price, doing the shooting himself and pocketing the difference.

Since they wouldn't let him use the steamers to transport nitro, he hired a crew of fishermen and their sailboat for the job, but he didn't tell them the cargo would be 1,000 quarts of high explosive from the Hercules Torpedo Company.

When they finally found out what he had on board, they were scared to death. The slightest jar could set the stuff off and blow them all sky-high. Nobody, including Frosty, himself, breathed easily until the boat docked and he got the dangerous cargo ashore.

The fishermen gave him and his schemes wide berth after this, but the lure of ready cash led him into one more transportation deal in late winter, which was also dangerous and could have gotten them all drowned.

When the lake was frozen over there was no way of reaching the mainland, as the ferry shut down. To get around walking 14 miles to land, they built an ice boat called the "Yankee," and learned how to sail it. This was great sport and when there was a good wind, the speed was "estimated" at 100 miles an hour.

The mail was brought over from Leamington by a sled boat pulled by a horse. One day in March the mail they expected did not come. There was no word from the syndicate and no money. Frosty and Tiny decided to go to Leamington, to wire the president and get matters straightened out. They started out at 6 a.m. one day, guided by a Boy Scout compass. When they got six miles out in the channel they had to abandon the ice boat, and walk the remaining eight miles to shore on glare ice, as the ice had heaved and left pressure ridges, cracks and cakes all over the ice surface.

They arrived at Ed Ryall's Hotel at 8 p.m., after being picked up and fed by a farmer. They knew Ryall as he had backed some of the Pelee Island wells.

They were surprised to find the bar full of old-time contractors and friends from the Findlay field. They had quite a reunion that night at the Huffman House, a hang-out for oil drilling types.

Even without hang-overs the next day, the pair would have found the news was bad. The syndicate had gone broke — and so were they. By nightfall, however, the story had changed.

On a previous visit to Leamington, Tiny and Frosty had come into contact with J.C. Hickey, of the National Supply Company. He told them one of the companies, in which Capt. Ed Winter and Ed Wigle were interested, was looking for somebody to drill a couple of wells near Leamington. They went around to see Winter and Wigle and before the day was over, made a deal under which the National Supply Company was to repossess the syndicate rig and turn it over to Tiny and Frosty. The whole clout of the deal was some 13-pound 6½-inch casing Frosty owned. The deal also included a $350 advance. Frosty also talked them into endorsing a note for an additional $350 operating loan at the bank.

The only problem now remaining was how to get the rig off the island. This called for ingenuity on their part, as the spring break-up was at hand. The Leamington teamsters they contacted would have nothing to do with them. It was too near break-up for their liking. They pointed out that Pelee had open water on both sides and, in case of a storm, they had little chance of surviving.

Tiny and Frosty walked home across the ice next day, arriving at 11 p.m. Despite the lateness of the hour, Frosty rousted out some of his fishermen friends who owned teams and sleighs and talked them into risking their necks on his behalf. They responded to that $350 in his pocket.

During the night they worked, breaking camp and dismantling the rig. The next morning, they began the most unorthodox entry of a drill rig ever to be found in oil history in Canada: a most hazardous trek.

The boiler was on one sleigh, the string of tools and casing on another, timber on the third and the derrick on the fourth — all overloaded, but easy sliding on the ice. Staring ahead apprehensively, they set out. The ice proved safe. It is noted in Tiny's scribbler:

"Everything went well until we came within a quarter mile of shore. There we ran into a five-foot wide crack in the ice. We solved the dilemma by cutting a large cake of ice and floating it into the gap, then laid planks across it. Somehow we got those loads across that unsteady bridge but it was tricky.

"We arrived at Leamington early in the evening. Being afraid the ice might break up at any time, the teamsters returned that night. Two days later the big break-up came."

The rig they ferried across the ice wasn't much to look at; their drilling pals ribbed them about having a "pile of junk." However, there was enough "junk" to drill three wells. But there was no lasting production in any.

Both men had had enough experience by this time that they could show their fellows a trick or two, especially when it came to water troubles in holes. Most of the holes were drilled into Guelph stratum. A peculiarity of this stratum was that water plagued drillers by rising in every hole. Various methods had been tried to stop the water without success.

However, Tiny devised a method of pulling up the casing and pouring four or five feet of concrete into the bottom of the hole. When set, the concrete effectively sealed off the water seepage. Then he would pound through the concrete plug and keep on drilling to pay dirt.

Chapter 4

Over Lake Erie Ice to Leamington

The Americans, in strait-laced Leamington, were looked upon with askance for their hard drinking and ebullient ways, by everybody except the kids.

They were heroes to the kids around town, especially on the Fourth of July, when they would give them 50 cents to buy firecrackers — bigger ones than most kids had ever been able to buy before with their pennies.

While the use of alcoholic beverages may be defensible on social grounds, it is indefensible when its use interferes with public safety. Elmer Selkirk, a former town clerk of Leamington, recalls how mixing nitroglycerine with alcohol resulted in the deaths of two oilmen. It was on a day when he and a chum played hookey from school to go to the Ira Rymal farm, to watch the drillers "shoot" a well.

Because of the peculiarities of the rock strata in the Leamington field, it was necessary to shoot nearly every well. This was a spectacle well worth any young fellow's time to stay off school, albeit it was a dangerous one.

When the drill had gone into the oil sand, (all kinds of rocks and soil strata were called "oil sand" by the drillers), it was frequently found the gas pressure was not enough to force the oil to flow through the pores in the rock, or that the rock was not sufficiently porous. In that case, a charge of nitro was sent down and exploded. This shattered the rock and almost invariably started the oil flowing.

The nitro was brought from the factory near town in square cans by teams and buckboards. On the side of the buckboards were two Ys, in which the cans were strapped. The reels for lowering and firing were carried behind. The buckboards were drawn over the rough roads at a fast pace, the drivers seemingly careless of the enormous power stored in the cans underneath them.

"The few car drivers of the time, used to give the well-known wagons a wide berth. They thought them dangerous," said Selkirk.

"When drivers saw one of them at a distance, they always seemed to think it convenient to go up the next concession, or to take the other side road."

Delivered to the well site, the nitro was poured into long thin cartridges or shells which, as a rule, held 10 quarts. Three, five, six or ten of these cartridges — according to the judgment of the shooter — were filled. Then, hooked to the end of the wire lowering line, the shells were slowly let down the casing. They were allowed to descend one on top of the other, in such a way that one fitted into the other. When each shell came to rest, the hook disengaged and the line reeled up. The lowest shell was supported up to the proper height in the sand, by a small tin tube called an "anchor."

The shooters had to be extremely careful in lowering the first shell; that it went to the proper place and had not stuck on some projection in the wall above where it was intended to be. It was necessary to use a measuring line to determine if the shell went down to the proper place.

There were several ways of exploding the nitroglycerine after it had been put into position in the well. The method in longest use was known as the "go-devil."

For a go-devil shot, the top shell had in its upper part a small perforated tin tube containing three or four little anvils, one above the other, each carrying a waterproof percussion cap. The nitroglycerine, when the shell was full, flowed in around these caps through the perforations in the small tube. On the upper cap rested an iron rod, fastened to a flat plate above the shell. When this shell was in place and the lowering line reeled up, an iron casting called the "go-devil" was dropped into the well. This falling weight struck upon the iron plate and the stock set off the percussion caps, expolding the nitroglycerine.

If the go-devil did not set off the shot because either it did not fall with sufficient rapidity through the salt water, or mud had fallen on the plate, the shot had to be "squibbed." The squib was a small shell, holding a quart or more of nitroglycerine. It was lowered until it rested on the shells in the well and was then fired, by letting a hollow weight run down on the wire line. Guided by the line, this weight struck a firing head similar to that used on larger shells and the explosion of the squib set off the larger bulk of nitroglycerine below.

When the charge was set off a dull thud was heard in the bowels of the earth. In a few moments, which seemed like hours, there was a resounding roar as the oil came rushing to the surface bringing with it water and whatever mud was in the hole. The resultant black spray often gushed high above the derrick.

The operation of filling the cartridges and devil-squib with nitro was always accompanied by a certain amount of risk, as this explosive is as easily ignited by friction as by percussion. For that reason, each cartridge was carefully washed off for fear that any liquid spilling over the sides and the cartridge rubbing against the side of the casing while being lowered into the well, could set it off prematurely.

It was by neglecting to do this, by a couple of devil-may-care American well shooters, who had a couple too many under the belt, that the hookey-playing adventure of Elmer Selkird and his pal, climaxed into one of horror.

"I guess they just didn't give a damn," he said. "All of a sudden there was a premature explosion and arms, legs and derrick timbers fell all around us as we stood and watched. I remembered that day all my life."

Accidents happened only once in the life of a high-explosives handler. Once was the last time. Nitroglycerine was especially tricky to handle. Fumes from the empty cans were the most dangerous of all. The "shooters" had a real fear of the empties.

The stuff would freeze in winter and had to be thawed out in barrels of hot water. This was an eerie, if not downright dangerous, job. (Handling of nitro has been eliminated today, since the practice of sand fracturing and the use of acid has become standard practice.)

Although carrying full cans of the explosive was the safest of all for the handlers, there was always the possibility that a hard jolt would set it off and blow everything sky-high.

Ice boat on Lake Erie at Leamington, Ontario.

Chapter 5

A Contract With Eugene Coste

Del Mullen was one of the survivors. He was a roistering well-shooter from the Ohio field. He had handled thousands of gallons of nitro in his career and had learned to live with it.

Art Robinson, a plumber, recalled how Mullen drove up in front of the shop one day and asked him to make six of the long tin cans, used to lower the nitro down the holes.

Art got busy and made them and took them out to the car. There he discovered that Mullen had 15 gallons of nitro in the back seat. One ripple and the stuff would have blown the town sky high. However, Mullen seemed unconcerned and drove away with it to the field.

Mullen was an intrepid practical joker. One of the stunts he used to pull, was to take a mouthful of coal oil and wait till he saw somebody go to light his pipe, then sidle up beside him and spew the coal oil from his lips in a fine spray.

It would blow up with quite a flash and bang — much to the amusement of the bystanders.

Mullen would then go to the nearest bar and take a slug of good Canadian whisky, to take the taste of the coal oil away.

Mullen's favorite yarns were about getting the better of the Findlay police, who tried to enforce a bylaw prohibiting transport of nitro on city streets. The bylaw resulted from an explosion in the city centre in which two men and two horses were killed.

Any attempt to arrest a driver, resulted in him getting off his wagon and offering the cop the reins.

That usually ended it. No cop was brave enough to take over the reins. And he would have been afraid to take the driver away and leave the wagon standing in the street. Most drivers were given warnings and allowed to go on their way.

But one of Mullen's mates had his bluff called by Constable Jack Crawford. When the driver got off the wagon, Crawford calmly took his place, picked up the reins and motioned the startled driver up onto the seat beside him and drove to the police station.

Crawford had been a nitro wagon driver himself. That ended those shenanigans.

The Leamington-Mersea oil field was a small one — only eight miles long and half a mile wide — brought in 1902. It was part of a larger field extending from Petrolia, (Canada's first commercial field), across the west end of Lake Erie to Findlay. It was also exploited for natural gas and marketable quantities sold by Eugene Coste, a native of Amherstburg, Ont. A man who was to have an enormous influence on the lives of Tiny and Frosty.

The original big players in the Leamington field were Capt. Ed Winter, a lake boat captain, and Ed Wigle, a crony of Winter and a partner with him in the Leamington Torpedo Company. They founded the Leamington Oil Company, in 1904, with capital raised by friends of J.C. Hickey of Detroit.

Hickey was associated with the National Supply Company, which supplied most of the drilling equipment in the United States and, from 1905, in Canada. Hickey also headed the Detroit Oil Exchange, where most of Ontario's venture capital was raised.

Hickey also formed an oil company, when Winter's company brought in a well with a good paying flow. The Winter well started an oil rush, which saw 300 technical personnel from the Ohio fields working there, in the summer of 1905. Common labourers in the oil fields of Ontario were making $2 to $5 a day, compared to $1 a day for industrial labourers.

When there was a slow day, the city editor of the Toronto Globe would assign a reporter to take the train to Leamington and do an update on the drilling. Those stories brought in thousands in new capital, as they indicated oil was flowing from gushers in all directions, because of lack of wooden tankage to contain it. But nobody cared — especially the farmers. They were collecting big royalties and becoming rich. And then, if the flow of a well was shut off, how would the well owners be able to tell if there was any more in the ground.

A note from Tiny's scribbler attempts to clear up a popular misconception, that has created hard feeling between eastern and western farmers even to this day.

Ontario farmers owned their own mineral rights and the usual lease rental was one barrel for every eight produced. In the three Prairie provinces, the provincial governments took over all mineral rights from the federal government in 1905, (except those owned by the Canadian Pacific Railway and the Hudson's Bay Company). The provinces thus collect the royalties and the land owners receive only a small rental from oil companies, for the use of their surface rights. Few people in the east believe farmers get such a shoddy deal.

In 1904, oil companies were receiving $1.86½ a barrel at the refinery in Sarnia. The refiners paid $1.34 a barrel and the federal government 52½ cents bounty. The bounty was paid to encourage drilling for oil, as the demand in Canada then made it necessary to import large amounts from the United States.

At the time, the U.S. was carrying out an intensive drilling program of 1,400 wells a month, while Canada was spudding in only 20, despite the royalty.

The politics of government intervention in oil pricing is interesting. The Canadian government subsidy didn't succeed in increasing supplies, because there wasn't much oil in Ontario for self-sufficiency in 1904. However, in the 1980s, the National Energy Program tax of the Trudeau government, nearly put the Canadian oil industry out of business in the West. This policy was a repeat of a five-cent-a-barrel tax, which Pennsylvania placed on its oil production, a tax which forced small producers out of business.

The bounty never had a chance to prove anything in the Leamington field as it petered out by 1910.

When Tiny and Frosty finished drilling three low-producing wells for Winter, work had started to become scarce. Thus, when Eugene Coste, the geologist for the Provincial Natural Gas and Fuel Company, offered them a contract to drill three wells at Dunnville, Ont., at the east end of Lake Erie, they moved there quickly.

These wells were part of a wildcatting program. Coste visited the rig while they were setting it up. He was disappointed in their equipment, which looked like all oil drilling outfits when piled on the ground: a pile of junk. He doubted they could drill a well with it.

However, they persevered and brought in a hole with a slight showing of gas. Coste sold the pipe in the hole to a farmer and the gas went to supply his home and a nearby school. Tiny wrote of Coste on page 18:

"I told him our pile of junk was all Frosty and I had to make our living. If we didn't think we could finish the contract, we wouldn't have taken it. Coste admired our spirit. He told us to go ahead and he'd consider what was to be done on the second hole. What he did was the biggest surprise of our lives.

"Although he was a professional geologist he had the common touch. He would come into a rig and look around and want to know everything. He asked questions to the point of annoyance to the crew. He was also quick-tempered and could get into a quarrel mighty fast. But he was admired and respected by the workers in the field. If he

Eugene Coste of Amherstberg, Ontario, the man with the "golden touch". Photo: Glenbow Archives, Calgary, Alberta.

came out and had to stay overnight and no extra cots were available, he would roll up in a blanket and sleep on the floor of the tent.

"He was a good man to be around as every project he touched made money. He had a golden touch."

The Costes were a remarkable family. Eugene was the third son of a Frenchman, Napoleon Coste of Marseilles, who went to sea but jumped ship at Amherstburg, Ontario. Here Eugene was born in 1859.

Four years later the family moved back to France, where the sons were later educated as professional engineers in Paris. The money to finance their education was made by Napoleon as a contractor on the Suez Canal, completed in 1869.

The family moved back to Amherstburg in 1882 and built Mireille, a large house that became a landmark. It was similar to Coste House built by Eugene in Calgary 30 years later, also a landmark.

Eugene went looking for gold in Ontario, then oil and gas. He brought some science to oil exploration, which had been previously based on the work of "witches" or dowsers.

His science was a bit different than the American and British school. He contended to his dying day, that oil and natural gas originated in inorganic or volcanic rocks. Mysterious fluids were created and they seeped into sediomentary formations where man could tap pools of them. The other view is oil and gas are of organic origin, living material which has been buried and compressed and congregates in underground pools.

Coste's first well was near Kingsville, Ont. It came in at 1,031 feet, with a flow of 10 million·cubic feet a day. His Prairie Natural Gas and Fuel Company exported gas to both Buffalo and Detroit. This continued until supplies became depleted by the turn of the century.

Back in Dunnville, Coste showed up at the second hole of Tiny and Frosty and asked them to break off and go to Langham, Saskatchewan, to a wildcat site on the North Saskatchewan River 20 miles northwest of Saskatoon. He had been retained by the railroad-building team of Mackenzie and Mann, to find oil to fuel the engines on the Canadian Northern Railway instead of coal. Oil would generally have speeded up the West's development. The year previous Coste had brought in a couple of Texas drillers with standard cable tools and they had run into trouble. They then persuaded him to buy one of the new rotary drills. It didn't work out; they twisted off three pipes and lost all their tools at the bottom of a 900-foot hole. Tiny and Frosty started over with cable tools.

Chapter 6

The Langham, Saskatchewan Adventure

The standard cable tool rig was invented at least 2,000 years ago, by the Chinese. They used it for drilling for salt water, to be evaporated to supply table salt. The chief changes made in the ancient contraption by the latter-day American drillers, was replacing the wooden tripod with a wooden derrick 40 feet high, (the height of the derrick was later doubled so that two lengths of 30-foot pipe could be handled at a time instead of one, and coolie labour was replaced by steam, (although early American and Canadian drillers for many years utilized manpower to "kick down" wells with spring pole tool outfits).

The cable tool outfit consisted of a derrick from which a long, chisel-nosed bit was suspended on a manilla rope line. The bit was a long heavy bar with its lower end dressed to a cutting edge. This was used to pound out a hole, as its weight broke or cut the stone where it struck. At each blow the bit was turned a little, making a round hole whose diameter is just the width of the cutting edge. It differed from hand drilling in a quarry, in that the drilling bar was not struck by any kind of a hammer. The drill, suspended from the end of the rope, was lifted for each stroke. The process was one of drilling, not one of boring, as it was sometimes called.

Steam power was used to raise the bit. After the drill had been working a while, the chips of rocks or drilling began to fill the hole and break the blow upon the solid rock. At intervals the driller was forced to pull his bit to clean the hole.

In some cases a sand trap could be used to clean out the rock and earth. However, the usual process was to pour in water and lift the fluid mud out with a long narrow baler with a valve at the lower end. These operations are alternated, first, drilling ahead five feet, then cleaning out the fine mud, drilling again and so on day and night till the desired depth has been reached. In the early days, each five feet of drilling was called a "screw."

Attached to the top of the bit were several kinds of weights and jars. The whole was called a "string of tools." Some of the strings later on were 60 feet long, as different attachments were added.

When the bit became dull, it was removed and another put in its place. The dull bit was heated red hot, the point reshaped with a 10-pound sledge and finally tempered by a tool dresser.

The cable rig has largely been superseded by the faster, bigger, more expensive rotary drill rigs.

Using rotary drills a well is bored into the earth by rotating a sharp hollow circular bit fastened to a string of connected drill pipe, which is revolved by a rotary table in the derrick floor. The draw works turns the table by a chain drive and can rotate more than 300 tons of drilling pipe, at the rate of up to 200 revolutions a minute.

The long string of drill pipe is hollow through its entire length, to permit the pumping through of chemically treated "mud," to flush out the cuttings of rock, lubricate the bit and contain the oil, gas and water pressures that are encountered. In a continous circuit from the mud tanks to the slush pumps to the fleixible hose, which introduces the mud into the pipe, the mud is pumped under high pressure through the bit, up through the space between the outside of the drill pipe and the wall of the hole and back to the tanks.

To facilitate coupling and uncoupling, since the drill string must be pulled out of the well many times to change bits or to insert a tubular lining of steel casing, the pipe is threaded together, usually in 30-foot lengths, which are added singly as the well deepens. The drill pipe is pulled out in sections and a section may range from one length to five lengths. It is the length of sections, by which pipe will be pulled out, that determines the height of the derrick. The tallest derricks are more than 200 feet high, as tall as a 15-storey building.

The drilling pipe actually "hangs" from the top of the derrick. The nerve centre of the rig is the draw works. This is essentially a powerful winch, with a huge drum on which the hoisting cable is spooled. From it the cable is strung through the sheaves of a crown block, at the top of the derrick and the suspended travelling block.

In the biggest derricks, the travelling blocks weigh seven tons, the hook four tons and the derrick's frame of prefabricated steel 40 tons. The derrick is built strong enough so it will hoist and control 40 tons.

An explanation about one of the dangers of gas drilling, especially in Alberta, from Tiny Phillips' scribbler:

"In the early days, the drillers often had inadequate tools to cope with high gas pressures. Control was necessary to prevent fires.

"When I would shut a gate on a well and see the pressure run up to 3,000 pounds per square inch — a pressure so high I couldn't open it by hand — I was about ready to run.

"At times the expansion pressure on the pipes would be so great that within the space of a minute they would become coated with ice."

When Tiny and Frosty left for Langham, Tiny's scribbler showed: "I had never heard of Saskatchewan and Alberta before — until Coste showed us the location on a map. He made an agreement to buy our drill rig and pay our expenses, from the time we left Findlay until we returned. The ironic part of this deal is we never returned to Findlay permanently.

"We took our wives but the only place for them in this small Prairie town, was a big boarding house which provided overnight accommodation for cow punchers and travellers. When the weather was still warm, they could live in a tent in the field but when it got cold, they had to move back to Langham.

"This big-sky country and its possibilities intrigued us. The people did, too. The most unique we ran into were the Doukhobors who were brought in from Russia by Interior Minister Clifford Sifton to colonize the West.

"But they would take off on religious pilgrimages, leaving their livestock to run loose. The radical Sons of Freedom sect were always protesting something or other. And the way they attracted attention to the cause, was to strip naked and terrorize people by setting fire to their homes.

"One husky Royal Canadian Mounted Police sergeant told me, one has never done a real day's work until he has tried to wrestle a naked 300-pound Doukhobor woman onto a CPR train to send the protesters home."

Tiny and Frosty worked on the well until the summer of 1906. Delays had been experienced in rail delivery of pipe. But when they reached the 1,358-foot depth and hadn't brought in oil, Coste closed down the job.

Chapter 7

29 Million Cubic Feet a Day

W*hen he* shut down this project, Coste had other things in mind for them. He asked them to go to Medicine Hat, Alberta, in the late summer of 1906, to work on a wildcat drilling contract for the Canadian Pacific Railway. Frosty became field superintendent and Tiny head driller. The culmination of this venture was the first big natural gas discovery in Alberta, when Old Glory was drilled near Bow Island in 1908-9. Oil was not found in commercial quantities here.

Generally lost sight of in this drilling project, was the fact a number of smaller commercial gas finds were brought in at Dunmore, Cummings, Suffield, Brooks and Bassano.

Their contract with Coste allowed Frosty and Tiny to do some freelance work. Between the time they arrived in Medicine Hat and the bringing in of Old Glory, they had drilled five gas wells for J.D. McGregor of the Grand Forks Cattle Company, who had an 80,000-acre grazing lease near Medicine Hat. This lease was later expanded to 380,000 acres through his participation in the Southern Alberta Land Company. His idea was to use cheap natural gas to operate huge pumps, to lift water 300 feet over the banks of the Bow and Belly Rivers to an extensive irrigation system, in this semi-arid short-grass prairie. He had been persuaded by Coste there was sufficient gas to achieve this purpose. There was — but the cable tool rigs were not capable of reaching enough of it to do the job.

McGregor toyed with the idea of tapping into larger constant gas reserves around Medicine Hat, but eventually the concept was dropped as there was no guarantee of continuity of supply.

Despite the failure of finding enough gas for this purpose, McGregor and the SAL continued the wildcat drilling program. Up to 1914, $127,000 had been spent.

From the very first he had pushed a scheme to build an electric railway from Medicine Hat to Calgary via Suffield, Ronalane, Retlaw,

*James Duncan McGregor
(1860-1935). Cattleman
extraordinaire who, in 1929
at the age of 69, was
appointed Lieutenant-
Governor of Alberta. Photo:
Western Canada Pictorial
Index.*

Milo, Arrowwood and Aldersyde. Once again he planned to use gas for power generation. The Phillips' scribbler notes:

McGregor and his brother, Colin, were obsessed about electric railways as a quick, effective means of transportation for farmers. At one point construction bonds had been guaranteed. Not only that, but a successful well was brought in on Colin's farm at 2,177 feet. On it were based the hopes of supplying power for the electric railway and for the proposed townsite of Ronalane nearby. Neither ever got past the planning stages. Later the CPR built a branchline over the right-of-way McGregor acquired.

That left him with quantities of gas, which were developed for heating homes.

When McGregor's grand idea didn't pan out, necessity sent the SAL 150 miles up the Bow River to build a diversion works at Carseland. Bow River water was sent coursing through an immense canal system; dumped back into the river at Ronalane.

Tiny and Frosty had more success in drilling under the CPR contract. Based on the success of the Colin McGregor well north of the river, they decided to drill for the CPR south of the river. But this project didn't happen immediately. The engineer of the western region of the CPR didn't take kindly to this idea, being a good company man with little imagination and a finely ingrained sense of job security.

Working for the CPR was usually akin to holding a civil service job, with attendant inter-department wars fought hand-to-hand. At that particular period in 1907, Guinter, the man in charge before Frosty arrived, decided to side with the engineer. The result was it was decided to drill another well at Dunmore Junction. Drilling here was regarded as a "sure thing" as gas had been discovered in Medicine Hat sand, which was very productive in the vicinity. An eight-inch pipe was drilled into this zone but it froze. It was then decided to abandon the well.

The rig was finally moved to the Bow Island location with a payroll which included Frank Lawler, Martin Hovis and Garrett W. Green, drillers; H.C. (Fat) Gloyd, Edward Cumming and Alvin Van Alst, tool dressers; Chris Haerman, T. Penhale, R.L. Quinn, H.C. Schouert, F. Hopkins, helpers; A.W. Chisholm and H. Blythe, teamsters; J. Fun, H. Hanson, T.A. McElhany, J.A. Rees, H. Arblaster, T.A. Ross and D.W. Angus, carpenters; M. Cumming and S. Kunerman, cooks; and Orville Fuller, Hugh Henderson, L.E. Exley, J.H. Brown, J.C. Bright, supernumaries with no fixed occupation.

The year was 1908. The well was officially known as Bow Island No. 1. But when it blew in at eight million cubic feet a day — the biggest gas well in Canada at that time — the American drillers dubbed it Old Glory.

In one of those crazy incidents which often precede big discoveries, Old Glory came within an ace of not being drilled on the site which brought in the hugh flow of gas. When Martin appeared on the job site, he found the derrick had been built and pipe and fuel were on the ground. Coste came out from his Toronto office on an inspection tour and, to his horror, found the crew had located the well on the wrong lease.

Due to a misunderstanding or just plain error — easy to make on the trackless open range — the crew had started work on Crown land, not CPR land.

Coste told Frosty to tear down the rig and move to the correct location. Frosty figured this was a sacrilege. He argued with him for a couple of days to let them go ahead and drill and straighten out the paper work later if need be. With plenty of misgivings Coste agreed reluctantly.

Of course, when the big well came in there was a great scramble in the CPR legal department in Montreal, to get the matter straightened out. The man sent to straighten things out was its young assistant solicitor, E.W. Beatty, (later to become company president).

He arranged for a swap with the Canada Department of the Interior for a quarter-section the CPR owned near Innisfail, a quarter that was later granted as a homestead to Gisli Erickson.

This seemed a simple enough transaction but legal minds wrangled over it several years before it was satifactorily settled in favour of the railroad.

The CPR owned all the land and mineral rights for 20 miles on each side of lines it built, as part of the compensation given it by the federal government for building the system linking Eastern and Western Canada. The big question mark was: Would the CPR secure the mineral rights under the Crown land on which Old Glory was located? If the interior department withheld the mineral rights, would it mean the CPR would be required to pay the government a hefty slice of royalties? It was finally established the CPR did own the mineral rights. The question never entered anyone's mind, that the mineral rights under Erickson's land might have been worth considerably more years later.

Drillers in the early days in the Canadian West had to know more than the physical end of operating the drill. They had to operate on guile and bravado along with their ability to "string along" their principals, who were usually far from the scene. The reason for this was, that trouble often developed during a drilling operation and the drillers operated on the theory that what the bankrollers didn't know, didn't hurt them. It was the custom to create a "bank roll" of their own by holding back in drilling reports a few hundred feet on the actual depth of the well, so that if trouble occurred progress could be reported while the trouble was being remedied.

Tiny's log of the well, in the well-thumbed scribbler, shows there was a great deal of trouble with the well. The CPR engineer in Winnipeg was told they were down only 900 feet, when they actually they were down 1,100.

Although most of the wells up to that time were producing from Medicine Hat gas sand, Tiny and Frosty were of the opinion if they could get down to Dakota sand, the flow would be greater. The only thing they didn't know was how deep they'd have to go to reach this formation.

At 1,860 feet, (actually only 1,660), they ran into real trouble when they lost some tools in the hole. They lost the under-reamer dogs and broke the stem of the six-inch bit in the lower weld. This required what is known in the trade as a "fishing job," a job at which Tiny became very proficient and won himself quite a reputation later in the Alberta oil fields.

They used up all the "bank roll" on the fishing job and Coste,

C.P.R. Oil well located on a siding at Brooks, Alberta, 1912. Photo: Glenbow Archives, Calgary, Alberta.

becoming wary of the progress reports, ordered them to abandon the well. This put them in a quandry, because they were surer than ever there was a big flow of gas in the hole.

It was well into the middle of January, 1909, by then. Contact with the East was rather indefinite. Frosty put his creative efforts to work writing long-drawn-out alibis and somehow two or three telegrams from Coste telling them to cease and desist, got lost in transit from the CPR station at Bow Island to the wellsite. The crew was drilling 24 hours a day. At 1,912 feet a great flow of gas estimated at 4½ million feet was encountered. Tiny exulted in his scribbler:

"I remember Old Glory came in on the daylight tour. It was spitting sand out of the hole after we had drilled a few feet into the Dakota formation. There was great jubilation that day for this was the first big producer in the new Province of Alberta."

They knew their job was done Feb. 17, 1909, when the flow of gas measured four million feet after the well had blown wide open a month. It was then decided to drill another few feet. This paid off. At 1,915 feet the flow increased to seven million. On Feb. 23 the flow increased to 8.3 million.

Coste forgave all. He wired them to tube the well. But this wasn't the end of the excitement at Old Glory. Big trouble occurred July 18 when a group of farmers visited the site.

"One of them, A. Tremblay, deliberately struck a match near a leaking gate valve to see what would happen. His assurance was highly volatile. Leakage was coming through a brand new four-inch

No. 2000 Darling gate valve, with a heavy four-inch plug screwed in the open end of the gate.

"It was a small leak and did not amount to anything. The fire could have been put out easily, if there had been anyone at the pumphouse who knew anything about gas. After the fire had burned a few minutes the heat began to expand the balance of the connections and fittings and caused gas to leak through them. The other leaks naturally caught fire and the gaskets started to burn in the gate valves. The heat was so intense the brass valves started to melt. Finally, the tubing became so hot it burst with the internal pressure of 800 pounds."

A drill crew was pulled off the Bassano well and sent to Bow Island with a couple of boilers, to make steam to smother the "nasty" fire. The heat was so intense a man couldn't get within 75 feet of the fire.

Frosty put in a request to a CPR vice-president in Winnipeg to send in an army unit with a 10-pound gun, to shoot the fiery valves off if the steam failed to douse the fire. Fortunately, the artillery wasn't needed. On July 28, Tiny was able to douse the fire with two boilers of steam.

In the early days, as many as 10 to 12 boilers were required to snuff gas fires. The object was to move the boilers as near to the fire as possible and to cut the oxygen supply by blowing live steam at 150 pounds pressure into the fire through 12-inch pipes. A large empty pipe laid on the opposite side of the well to the boilers was laid to "pull the flame into it."

If Old Glory was considered a big well, Bow Island No. 4 was considered the granddaddy. It came in at 29 million cubic feet. All the adjectives were gone by the time No. 6 came in at 42 million.

Those wells assured Coste that field had sufficient reserves to take on the Calgary market 170 miles away and supply it by pipeline. At its height the total field totalled 59 million cubic feet a day at a pressure of 800 pounds.

History must record that the chronicle of the discovery and development in the natural gas industry might have been written quite differently, had it not been for the brassy intestinal fortitude of a couple of young American drillers, with a shirttail full of equipment (by present-day standards), and nothing to lose and who kept drilling at No. 1 well against all odds and orders. There is no gainsaying that luck played a part. The result was that it ensured them of jobs, as Coste went East to arrange for the financing to drill more wells to prove up the Bow Island field. Tiny's scribbler records:

"I often think of the loyalty of the men in this industry, who were willing to go into those rigs where oil and salt water were spraying many feet above the top of the derrick. They were ready to go up the rig, clad in oilskin suits and rubber hats and boots and take their turns in putting tubing into the wells. They could only endure about 20 minutes at a time of this kind of punishment. But it had to be done. In spite of all obstacles, the wells were eventually tubed in with a rock pressure of more than 1,200 pounds.

"In my job, even though I worked a 12-hour day, my work was never done Maybe I would have a Sunday off — or a weekend. But then the next week it meant going day and night no matter what the weather.

"Often it meant barreling across the prairie in an open car, with the side curtains flopping in the wind in a blizzard or at 25 below zero. You just had to get that gas or oil well going.

"Maybe you were moving to a new location and your boiler didn't show up. You would go down the road a mile or two and hear your teamster cussing the horses, because they couldn't pull the load out of a mudhole. Maybe after a futile attempt to move a heavy wagon he would have to unhitch, arrive at camp at 8 p.m., feed the tired teams and slide into a bunk for a few hours of sleep.

"Next morning the teamster would be up before dawn and go back to the load with a new idea for moving it. Maybe it would move this time.

"When I first started drilling I often slept on the ground wrapped in a blanket after following a rutted wagon trail all day. There were bountiful trout streams, numerous elk, deer, bears, with wolves and coyotes to keep you awake at night with their howls.

"That is the pioneering work I and my good fellows did for our newly adopted province. You wonder at times that some of the brass of the government, who brag about the riches of the Province of Alberta, have the nerve to brag. They never went through what the common drillers, tool pushers, roustabouts and other labourers did to bring in the volume of oil and gas which has filled government coffers so full of money, they are now fighting about the way it is being distributed.

"Yes, this is a rich province. Thanks to who?

"But the compensations were the many trips through snowcapped mountains and green valleys. What more could a romantic person wish for?"

While this is a noble sentiment, the real facts of the matter are, that drillers weren't making all that much and they had to improvise and cut their living costs by any means possible.

For instance, when Tiny was drilling Old Glory winter came early in 1908, he and Zulah and their 18-month-old son, Fred, were living in a tent at the wellsite. It was customary in those early days, for the families to go to camp along with the men. They lived in tents with board floors. These provided good, snug, warm living conditions until the bitter cold weather came.

Zulah used to talk about an early November storm that blew in and piled so much snow around the tent, the men from another tent had to come and dig them out in the morning. Following that, the families moved to a Medicine Hat apartment for the winter.

The prairies were just being opened to the big wave of settlers at the time and Zulah recalled seeing plenty of buffalo skulls along the wagon roads. When one had to travel off the wagon roads, the only means of finding the way from one place to another was the odd survey marker. It was a delight for the women to arrive in Medicine Hat and find concrete pavements.

There were Indians encamped in the vicinity who delighted young Fred with the mocassins they made for him and who couldn't fathom just what the palefaces from the CPR were up to, with their giant rig.

The Phillip's early days in the West were in the age when homesteaders made a bet of $10 with the government, that if they could stick to a quarter-section three years it was theirs. But a good many did not make it — after working two years for nothing.

The only thing necessary to get one's hands on the 160 acres, was to file on the homestead at the land office, then hunt out the corner-stake — no easy task. This was a country where one would see for miles in all directions with nothing but blue sky, hot sun and heat coming up in waves; maybe a few head of cattle belonging to some other homesteader five or six miles away. There was no fencing in sight. A note in Tiny's scribbler:

"You wondered who the land belonged to: a rancher or the government? But the rancher was there. So what?

"It was up to you to make a country of this province of Alberta.

"Many people emigrated without much and expected to get rich by work alone. But they did not always succeed. The authorities told them they had to build a house on a homestead pre-emption, before they could claim the land for $10. Many a poor fellow built the house out of sods and lived that way maybe the first year, maybe two.

"The settlers would try to make enough out of the crops to build the obligatory house, but in many years the crops withered in the drought. It was so dry water would have to be hauled for the livestock from a slough or a buffalo wallow. Even then, many did not make it and had to move off the land.

"Fortunately I had other things to do than try to establish myself that way."

Tiny was in a business where there were heartbreaks and erratic tool deliveries from the eastern United States, few experienced and reliable drilling personnel, (many a worker became a contractor overnight), little reliable geological data, too little capital, most of the equipment carried 37% duty and roads practically nonexistent.

However, the courage and tenacity of the early-day drillers in holding on and muddling through is paying off for succeeding generations.

But that is the way with pioneering ventures. The people who take the risks make the least out of them. Despite the insecurity and instability of the new industry in its formative years in this country, it is one of the most solidly based businesses in the industrial complex now. From 20-25 per cent of the population, are directly dependent on oil for its livelihood.

Sixty years ago an anonymous writer penned a florid tribute to the oil driler which is appropriate now:

The driller, he of the brood with the mile-long feelers.

It was the driller who made the petrocrats.

Read of and conceived in fancy the men who piled rocks. Great rocks on polygonal bases in the valley of the Nile, somewhere in the dead dim ages of the past. Clothe, crown and sceptre them with divinity. Put all the sun-up, sun-down and moon-flame glory into their mantles of accomplishment, if you will, then trot them out inside the oil-bespattered driller and compare.

Know ye that it was the driller with his oblong feelers that caverned the earth and solid rocks, found and harpooned the age of oil and flung it up and over the earth. He did that and none else. Without him this gorgeous age of oil — this more — than imperial glory with which it fills the world — would still be asleep down there.

Think of it:

Without him the hammer of the tool dresser would be unheard. The praise of the superintendent for his great success in bringing in the last well would be as a shake of the head unshook. Without the driller, Rockefeller might be named Smith the bullwhacker, and Standard Oil a peddler of cure-alls bottled from oil springs.

There is none in the great productive game who has so much financial responsibility resting directly upon his shoulders, as the driller of oil wells. A miscatch of sound, slip of hand, waver in decision and $100,000 is dropped into a mile-deep hole never again to be fished up. Such a man must have nerve as well as brains and must be every inch a commander or he is lost. It is the driller who makes or unmakes the success in the oil business, all things being equal. The man who starts in production and does not know a driller when he sees him, has already the maximum show of failure in his undertaking. There are men who drill, plenty of them, but they are not drillers. Ask the boys and they will tell you so. The driller is a thorough, practical man — must be necessarily so because there are no books or formulae for him to study, no technical schools from which he may graduate. He must learn by experience. The oil driller must have the rope knowledge of a sailor, the essential points of good blacksmithing, some of the fundamentals of a machinist, carpenter, architect, plumber. He must possess the rhythm of mechanics, the grasp of physics and the patient deductive power of an astronomer.

Chapter 8

British Investment in Bow Island Gas

There was an element of danger in the drilling business. It was during the drilling of a SAL well that Tiny Phillips experienced one of the first big gas field fires in Alberta. His crew was working on a well which had come in at 14 million feet a day at 500 pounds. It began to blow out tons of chirt or flint pebbles. The company had decided to tube the well with four-inch pipe in the six-inch hole to shut it off. The situation was extremely dangerous for the crew, as only one pebble hitting the steel block or elevators could spark a fire that would blow them all sky-high.

At noon one day, during the tubing operation, they quit at noon and walked to the cook shack, 2,00 feet from the rig. Just as they arrived there was a great roar. Fire and flames were shooting out the top of the 72-foot derrick.

The crew could do nothing but sit down on the hillside and watch everything burn up. They were all weak-kneed and had the same thought: it wasn't their time to go that day.

Frosty wasn't there at the time. He was in hospital with a bad burn he had suffered a few days previously. It took a week to put out the fire: Tiny's first — and nothing to fool with. The rig was rebuilt and it took another two weeks to get the gas shut off for good.

Frosty's accident occurred at Redcliff, when he tried to light a cigar and escaping gas ignited. He lay on the ground and directed the extinguishing of the fire with steam. Then he drove his own car to hospital for treatment. Persons in most industries in the 1980s, are always surprised to hear of the low expenses of the pioneers. In the oil patch, $100 to $150 a month plus board for drillers and $100 a month for tool dressers, enabled Martin and Phillips to drill successful wells for as little as $25,000.

With such relatively low wages, most workers were always looking around for money-making opportunities. It was therefore easy for Coste to hire Frosty for $200 a month, to go out on the road to sell gas franchises to municipalities. The first city administration he talked to was Lethbridge for gas at 25 cents per 1,000 cubic feet.

Since Lethbridge was a coal-mining town there was a great deal of opposition. The pair therefore bypassed Lethbridge and went for the larger Calgary market. They found prospects good — even though there were already two gas companies serving this city of 30,000. It took them a long time to deliver gas to the city. The big stumbling block was the board of directors of the CPR, 2,000 miles away.

For the next couple of years they learned why every Prairie farmer, at the mention of "CPR", raised his fist and mouthed the perennial oath: "Goddam the CPR."

The sticking point was that CPR had been looking for oil to fire its engines. Gas was an anathema to it and the directors were reluctant to exploit its sale. There was one main hold-out, E.W. Beatty. The rest didn't believe gas could be piped 170 miles, even though oil had been carried distances of more than 300 miles in the United States.

Even Sir Herbert Holt, named a director in 1911, had reservations about Coste's scheme being workable. If there was one who should have been Coste's ally it should have been Holt. He not only was an engineer by profession, but was president of the Montreal Gas Company. He had done his share of pushing through "unworkable" projects in his time.

Born in Dublin in 1856, he came to Canada and worked as a civil engineer on the Credit Valley Railroad in Ontario, (it was later taken over by the CPR and is the main line between Toronto and Windsor). He later became engineer and superintendent for the prairie and mountain divisions of the CPR, in 1883 and 1884.

Critics of the early construction which he undertook said a railway could never operate through mountains in winter. But the engineering was so well done CPR trains negotiated the Rockies year-round without any insurmountable difficulties.

His reputation as an engineer established, Holt got out of the construction field in 1901 and reorganized and became president of Montreal Gas. This put him on the rails as one of Canada's greatest financiers. He became a millionaire and president of Montreal Light, Heat and Power Consolidated.

Holt was of the opinion that pumping stations would be needed to push gas through and that, in winter, it might freeze in the pipeline. Coste and Martin argued that if pipes of large enough diameter were used this would not happen. They were correct, as it was later proven.

But in another of the amazingly stupid corporate decisions which plagued the CPR for many years, Thomas Shaughnessy's board turned down Coste's proposition — and ordered all wells capped.

Shaughnessy had 1½ years to decide what to do with the capped wells — so the dynamic little bearded Coste could only sit and await the board's pleasure.

The two companies supplying heating fuel to Calgary were:

The Calgary Gas Company, which was controlled by Pat Burns, the pioneer cattleman, meat packer, senator and millionaire. It manufactured gas and sold it for $1.50 per 1,000 compared to natural gas at 30 cents or less.

The Calgary Natural Gas Company was organized by Archibald W. Dingman. He was a principal in Pugsley, Dingman and Co. The company's Comfort soap plant in Toronto burned down in 1902, and he came to Calgary. As he had experience in the Pennsylvania oil fields, he organized a company to drill gas wells and set about to undersell Burns. He nearly succeeded, too, but ran out of money. A city bylaw to give him $10,000 failed — so he made a deal with the CPR to get more. The wells William Elder drilled for him could not supply the volume of those of Coste, despite his assurances to the contrary.

The CPR sent Frosty Martin around to check him out. Dingman kicked Martin out. Martin went back at night and measured the principal well, at what is now Inglewood Bird Sanctuary in East Calgary. He reported Dingman was lying. Therefore the CPR withdrew its support from Dingman and went back to Coste.

With the help of W.J. Kelly, a former associate in the development of natural gas in Ontario and a friend of Shaughnessy, Coste finally negotiated a deal with the CPR to sell its gas interests in the Bow Island field to a new company he organized, Prairie Gas Fuel Company. Under the deal the CPR got a royalty on every 1,00 feet of gas sold from its wells.

Coste and J.D. McGregor sought the assistance of an old friend, Clifford Sifton, to go to England to seek $7½ million to finance the company.

The remarkable efforts of these three Ontario neighbours proved invaluable in early developments in the Canadian West. Coste and McGregor were born in 1859 and 1860 respectively, in Amherstburg and Sifton first saw the light of day 115 miles away at Arva, just north of London, in 1861. Their paths crossed in many successful ventures. But this particular quest was a notable failure in The City, London England's financial district. They returned empty-handed from the first trip for two reasons:

1. The English financial nabobs had never heard of the Prairies.
2. They were unfamiliar with natural gas.

The rejection did not deter the fiery Coste. He returned to Canada and, on the advice of an English underwriter, changed the name of the company to "Canadian Western Natural Gas, Light, Heat and Power Co. Ltd." There could be no doubt now in the minds of the English investors where their money was going. A new charter was

Sir Clifford Sifton, Liberal MP Brandon (1896-1911): Minister of Interior, Superintendent of Indian Affairs; owner of Winnipeg Free Press for over 20 years. Photo: Western Canada Pictorial Index.

granted July 11, 1911 and the issue sold out immediately.

Pat Burns realized what was happening with this development and assigned his Calgary Gas Company franchise to Coste's new company — a deal worked out by a prominent Calgary lawyer, W.H. McLaws, and Frosty Martin.

Dingman went away mad and stayed mad at Frosty for a long time — a rivalry that continued during the later development of the well-known Turner Valley oilfield.

With the signing of this agreement, the city utility department wasted no time in giving the franchise for gas supply to Coste's company. Frosty teamed up with McLaws and they went on the road signing up supply franchises for 16 other municipalities along the line, including Lethbridge. The opposition was overcome in Lethbridge when Coste lit a gigantic gas flare just outside the city, for three days before the vote. The undecided decided to vote in favour and it carried by 17 votes. And the gas was sold for 35 cents — 10 cents above the original contract agreement.

Martin was put in charge of receiving and distributing the 50,000-ton order of pipe, supplied to the project by U.S. Steel Corp.

With the gas company well under way, Frosty could have stayed on as a salaried employee at a desk job. He chose to quit and become a millionaire. He and Tiny spudded in at Calgary and raised enough money to start a foundry in Medicine Hat in 1912.

Long after they had left the Bow Island field, it made oil patch history in another respect. By 1930, its producing days were ended after 336 billion cubic feet had been extracted. By then Canadian Western had developed new fields. It converted Bow Island into the first commercial storage field in Canada. Gas is piped to the wells in summer and drawn out to meet peak winter loads.

Coste and his family lived in their imposing 28-room house in Calgary's Mount Royal area until 1921 when, for a reason that remains conveniently forgotten by those Calgarians who know, he suddenly dropped his seat on the gas company board, sold his interests and moved back to Toronto.

The house stood empty for years and in 1947 the city took it over for $7,000 in back taxes. This bit of ignominity was unknown to Coste as he had died in 1941 at age 81.

Chapter 9

Medicine Hat — All Hell For a Basement

*F*rosty Martin had come to settle in Medicine Hat permanently in 1906. Also at the behest of Coste, Tiny Phillips had followed the next year.

The Martin family created a bit of a social stir in the community by bringing in from the United States a black mammy, Sarah, for their new son, Spud, born in 1912.

Frosty also owned the first Stutz Bearcat car in "The Hat."

A favourite story from the great scribbler concerns this car:

Martin was driving a Colonel Blimp-type Englishman across the prairie to inspect a wellsite. Although there was no road he got the car up to 60 miles an hour. It was the fastest ride the Englishman had ever experienced. He became a bit queasy but, not wanting to show his fear and keeping a stiff upper lip, he looked over at Frosty and said:

"I say, old chap, I don't know where we're going but we shan't be long, shall we?"

The Englishman no doubt recovered his equilibrium when Frosty stopped at the Elks Club, of which he and Tiny were charter members, for a double. Or it could have been the men-only Cypress Club, a distinction it still retains, despite onslaughts by the Status of Women Action Committee.

And again from the scribbler:

"Prior to my arrival my knowledge of the city was pretty scanty. I had a notion, like others around Findlay, that it was in the Far North and a terribly cold place to live. And it was that winter, too, because below-zero blizzards had wiped out about 45 per cent of the open-range cattle herd.

"At that time the U.S. Weather Bureau used to pick up a daily temperature report from Medicine Hat. When it turned cold there we noted that within three or four days our temperature dipped as did the temperature in areas all around the Great Lakes. We weren't as well informed about weather systems as we are today, to know most weather systems move from west to east in Canada."

"Zulah said that when we told people in Findlay we were moving to Medicine Hat, they were horrified. They thought we'd be going to the end of the earth and somehow might fall off."

A saying developed in the East that "Medicine Hat is the place where we get all our cold weather from." This infuriated the climate-sensitive Hatters: being on the edge of the Chinook belt, the winter temperature there moderates reasonably when the warm dry air blows in periodically. For several years they tried — unsuccessfully, to have the weather forecasters drop the temperature listing from their city. This failing, a faction in town sought to have the name of the city changed. This faction was joined by another group — mostly new-comers — who thought the name was undignified. They put pressure on city council to hold a plebiscite on the question.

The Establishment of the city, whose headquarters is the Cypress Club, were alarmed over the situation. They would be damned if they would allow the conformists to take over the city, especially since it had a non-conformist name if there ever was one. They hit upon the novel idea of writing to Kipling and asking for his advice.

Kipling, the noted British author, put Medicine Hat on the map for the English-speaking world when he blew into town in 1907. The drillers lit a giant gas flare for his amazement. His description of the friendly Western city was memorable: "It has all hell for a basement."

Kipling obliged the boys from the Cypress Club with a long essay which added up to, "no don't change your unique name." His clincher was: "What should a city be rechristened that has sold its name: Judasville?"

Needless to say Medicine Hat stuck.

As did Kipling, Tiny Phillips, found Medicine Hat a "Wonderful place" — once he got used to the cold. The warmth and easy way of life of the breed of people who inhabited the city and district, offset the coldness of the atmosphere. His first real introduction to the country "where the latchstring is always out" was New Year's Day, 1907. He unloaded his trunk at the CPR station and asked the agent where the customs officer was, as he wanted to clear it.

"He told me to go over near Arthur Burns lumber yard across the tracks and I would find the agent there curling. Burns had a sheet of ice in the yard and the curlers were sliding rocks around the ice," said Tiny.

Tiny found the customs officer but he was too busy curling to go clear the trunk.

"I told him I wanted my trunk and he asked me if I had a piece of paper. I handed him an envelope and he wrote on it: 'Please give

Phillips his trunk,' and went on curling. I went back to the station agent and had no trouble getting my trunk. That was when people were people and trusted you. They were happy and contented.

"Every homesteader or rancher for miles around knew everybody else and practised real Western hospitality. They would never let you go without staying a while and usually for a meal."

Medicine Hat was no stranger to gas when the Findlay drillers arrived. Attempts had been made on and off to develop gas for heating since 1901, even though the presence of gas had been detected 15 years earlier than that.

The discovery came about as another of those flukes which often characterize the search for natural resources: the search for one often leads to something more valuable. In Medicine Hat's case, the original search was for coal.

Up to that time, the CPR had not discovered any extensive source of coal for its Prairie lines and was hauling most of its supplies from the U.S. via the Lakehead.

Early in 1891, there were rumours afloat the CPR intended to move its repair shops from Medicine Hat. A committee from the Board of Trade waited on Sir William Van Horne, the president, as he stopped in the city on one of his annual inspection tours and asked if anything could be done to prevent the removal.

Van Horne assured them there was nothing to the rumour.

The city was so situated, he assured the committee, it would always be necessary to keep a considerable staff there. Further — and this was a spur to the delegation — as business increased so would the staff increase.

He pointed out if a good quantity of coal could be found under the city it would be useful to the railway. He suggested the Board of Trade spend some money to find out. He offered to loan a drilling rig for test work.

Test drilling was carried out that year along the south bank of the South Saskatchewan River. It established that coal was not present in commercial quantities but there was a good showing of gas at 660 feet. In fact, the city was sitting atop a huge gas field whose dimensions were not known. There were indications the supply was large, as youngsters skating on the river chopped holes in the ice and lit the gas which flared out of them.

The CPR already knew there was gas in the area as, in drilling water wells at stations to supply its steam engines, it had encountered gas. Attempts were made to utilize this gas at stations and section houses by employees. This source of heat was discontinued as there were too many fires and injury with it. They soon went back to wood and coal.

However, when the Canadian Northern started looking for oil to fire its engines, as seen previously, the CPR took up the search around Medicine Hat, as it was generally believed where there was gas there would be oil also. It was easy for Eugene Coste to break his contract with the financially shaky Canadian Northern and take on the CPR contract for oil exploration. He had also been approached by the Medicine Hat administration for supplying consulting services for its gas utility. With Frosty Martin now a permanent resident of the city he took over this function at $50 a month as, under the CPR contract, freelancing was permitted.

For the CPR contract the Martin-Phillips duo brought to Alberta a number of their friends from Findlay. This was the case at the Bassano well, where the CPR also had under way a huge dam to divert water from the Bow River for its Eastern Irrigation District, another huge land settlement scheme. Bassano was the jumping-off spot for hundreds of settlers heading north to the Red Deer River country.

The town had capitalized on the slogan coined by an innkeeper: The Best in The West By A Damsite. It provided a snicker in barrooms across the West.

Karl Karg Klentsche was one of the Findlay drillers. He came in 1909, moved to Calgary in 1928, to a house in Tiny's neighborhood and resided there until his death in 1964.

There was nothing in the way of a permanent population and nobody paid too much attention to the drillers. They were too busy with other things.

Klentsche was the archetype of the early hard-working, loud-swearing, hard-drinking, cigar-chomping boomer oil driller. At the age of 11, his stern German butcher-father took him out of school and put him to work driving a team, which he was doing when the famous Karg well turned Findlay into a boom town. Karg was young Karl's great-uncle.

The whole family moved to take advantage of the prosperity created by the boom. His father put several teams in the oil fields hauling tools, pipe and other supplies.

Klentsche used to claim the poor horses had the brains in his outfit, as he was too young to have many then. It was not unusual to see husky young teamsters of his age on the driver's seats of hundreds of wagons.

At age 13, he proved to be so adept with the reins he was hired for real cash money by his uncles to deliver meat. The job required him to be around at 6 a.m. and work till late at night "but they paid big money — all of $2 a week."

It was inevitable that after a year or two, he went into the drilling game where there was more money for a husky lad. He learned under

Old Man Butts, Tiny's step-father, (Tiny's mother had remarried).

It wasn't long before a gas-drilling program in Ontario called for a man of his experience. He went because "we jumped from place to place just like foxes, to wherever we could get the most money. There weren't too many of our breed then and we could afford to be snooty."

Klentsche moved around Alberta a great deal after Bassano — and he continued drilling till well after age 70, mostly on cable tool outfits.

One of the places he "jumped to" was Brooks, where he was the head driller who brought in a CPR well there. One day Frosty paid a visit and gave him a bawling out for something he figured wasn't right. Klentsche let him go until he had a skinful, then he lit into Frosty and told him off.

Klentsche expected to be canned for the outburst but Martin just looked at him and said, "If you can talk like that to people you should be able to boss men. At least, you have enough mouth to be head driller." And that's how he was promoted from second tour-driller to head driller.

Klentsche admired Frosty for two reasons: "He could drink anyone under the table with anything that had a kick in it. But I never saw the old bastard drunk." In later years, any of his friends who visited his office in Long Beach, Calif., could count on having a drink shoved into their hands. He kept his cabinet full all the time.

"The other characteristic we all admired, was that he never asked anybody to do anything he wouldn't do himself. He was a born leader."

Another Findlay driller was Martin Hovis. At first, he came during the summers only as he couldn't find year-round work. His name was to have a permanent place in Alberta's oil patch, as he was the head driller on the Dingman discovery well in Turner Valley in 1914.

Another trait that made him famous was that he practised his religion on the job. He quit several wells in protest over the amount of drinking taking place. This teetotaler would rather disassociate himself completely with a hard-drinking crew, than compromise his religious principles.

Still another driller who worked alongside Tiny and Frosty in the Turner Valley field was Roy Widney. He was born in Doylesburg, Pa., a little later than each of them — in 1885 — the son of a pumpkin farmer.

At age 21, he visited his cousin in California and came into a drilling job in the Kern County field near Bakersfield. Drilling had passed its pioneering stage by then in the U.S. and was emerging as a more scientific method of going through rock to oil sands. Some excellent drillers had risen to prominence and were his teachers.

In the six years he was in the field, he became one of the top cable tool drillers. But by 1912, over-production had shut down drilling.

He was a reliable driller who often worked 10 months without missing a shift. Thus, he usually had a fair nest egg stored away somewhere. He was urged by one of his co-workers to head for Alberta to look for some cheap land. The CPR was advertising heavily in the United States, for settlers to place on its land holdings.

"I came to Calgary and stopped at the old Wales Hotel in the fall of 1912," Widney said. "In the winter, a CPR land agent took me out in some of the sparsely settled areas by horse and cutter, to look for the kind of land I wanted. A couple of times we got pretty cold, when we couldn't find a place to stay until late at night.

"However, the search came to nought. I wanted two sections with a clear area two miles long that would lend itself to cultivating with tractor-drawn implements. The CPR couldn't produce it."

The CPR's loss was the Alberta oil patch's gain. Hanging around Calgary, he was contacted by two ranchers, William Livingstone and Joe Pugh of Okotoks, who had organized Southern Alberta Oil Company and were looking for a driller. Widney went to work for this company, half a mile south of Whisky Row and a mile south of the Dingman well.

He claimed to be the only survivor who got in on the ground floor, in the Turner Valley field and emerged with any lasting benefits.

From wildcat driller, he was able to go on and become one of the few self-made men in that oil patch. Most of the others gambled and lost or sold out to larger interests in later years. One of his nest eggs enabled him and his son, Dan, to go into the well-servicing business — and it was successful. He was able to retire in 1963, as president of Widney Oil and Drilling Co. Ltd. of Edmonton, with 20 well-servicing rigs.

Widney was right on the scene when the Dingman well came in. At that time, the Southern Alberta well was down only 600 feet. But it came in late, in the fall of 1914, with 40 to 50 barrels a day which was more than the Dingman production. It yielded enough oil to allow them to start a small refinery to produce naphtha, to sell to farmers in the area to operate their cars and tractors. The well was later sold to Imperial Oil.

It is characteristic of all drillers to be braggarts, to assume anything they did was done better or faster than anyone else. Widney could hold his own with any of them — and usually made his word stick.

During his California apprenticeship, he learned the knack of hooking "junk" stuck in a hole thousands of feet deep. Not a few drillers who regarded themselves as top men, were chagrined by his uncanny dexterity with fishing tools.

The classic among fishing jobs was one he did for the owners of Illinois No. 1, near Little Chicago, a suburb of Turner Valley. It had been shut down for six weeks with two bits in the hole. At least half a dozen other drillers were unable to recover them.

Widney received permission to shut down the well he was drilling and, for $20 a day and a stock issue, he tackled the fishing job. He pulled out the first bit in less than a day. The second one took longer — and drilling immediately resumed.

Stock in the Illinois had been trading at less than $1 a share. When the oil patch learned he had come onto the job to take charge of the fishing, the stock recovered its downward slump and went up to $4 a share. He, of course, was one of the shareholders who cashed in on the price rise.

During the second flurry of excitement in Turner Valley after 1924, he was a toolpusher on four wells drawing full salary for each — for a total salary of $2,500 a month. This lasted for three years. However big that money looked, he husbanded it well, because he knew he was in an unstable occupation with periods of inactivity. The family was thrifty and always grew a big vegetable garden. The flock of chickens always provided them with extra eggs, to be taken to the general store to trade for groceries.

Although he was willing to invest his money in the industry, Roy Widney sunk only one well on his own behalf. In partnership with several Calgary business men, he sank Widney No. 1 in 1929. It came in but there was no sale at the time for the product. He capped the well and held it for some time, until his partners prevailed upon him to pull the pipe and sell it. He pulled it three months too soon, as it could have been sold to one of the large companies buying production.

Widney pulled up stakes in the valley in 1918, when drilling just about came to an end due to the war. He intended to go back to California but never quite made it. A Vancouver promoter had a well in trouble at Langley. Some drillers had started down with a water-well drilling outfit and were getting nowhere. Off and on till 1924, he kept this hole going down to 7,500 feet, at which depth it came in with a small flow. At that time this was the deepest hole in Canada.

Chapter 10

Joseph Grant; Frosty and Tiny's Nemesis

The first attempts at providing gas for the citizens of Medicine Hat were carried out by a merchant, J. Charles Colter, before the turn of the century. He had drilled a small well near the first one discovered, when the Board of Trade was looking for coal for the CPR and found gas instead. His neighbors were so much impressed with the cheap and clean fuel they asked to be hooked up. In hooking up the Dr. Charles E. Smythe residence, he had to bury the pipe under the street.

Other private concerns made application to city council for a gas franchise. However, many citizens believed gas should be handled by a public utility.

A vote was held and a public utilities board was set up. To curb "freelancers" like Colter, a bylaw was passed that only the PUB could cross the streets with gas lines.

Tenders were called in 1901 for the drilling of enough wells to supply the city's needs. The contract was won by a Walsh rancher, Joseph A. Grant.

Grant is an almost-forgotten player in the Alberta oil patch. He was the man who provided the decisive push that initiated the province's commercial oil and gas industry. Although not the first to realize there were large quantities in the area, he was the first who showed it could be brought up in commercial quantities.

He had oil fever in his blood. When recurring bouts took him, Grant dropped everything else to go sink a hole somewhere. He first contracted the "bug" in the southwestern Ontario fields and never shook it off. His story was put on record by his son, Roy, at the old family home at Walsh in 1964:

Joe Grant was born at Kingston, Ont., in 1849. He graduated from the Royal Military College, married into a socially prominent family in 1870 and wanted to take a commission in the old Royal North West Mounted Police. However, his bride persuaded him against this idea as she did not relish life on the wide-open frontier country, with an

*Joseph A. Grant. Born at
Kingston, Ontario, Grant is
an almost forgotten player in
the Alberta oil patch. Glenbow
Archives, Calgary, Alberta.*

incipient Riel rebellion in the making. The RNWMP lost a good man,
for Grant was a strapping 5 feet 11 inches and weighed 200 pounds.

He settled for the relatively tame pursuit of agriculture at Corunna,
Ontario. In 1877, he went into the oil business at Oil Springs, Ont.,
and did well in that pioneer Ontario field. For several years he was
the reeve of Oil Springs. In 1884, the year Roy was born, he decided
to leave the oil business as he could foresee the gradual decline of
the field. He had decided to go back to the farm. Not even a
directorship in the new Imperial Oil Company could tempt him from
this decision.

In 1890 his brother, Frank, another RMC graduate and Great Lakes
sailor, persuaded him there were more opportunities for young men
in the West than in Ontario. Accordingly, they struck out and
eventually landed in Salt Lake City. Opportunities in real estate looked
good there and Frank went into the real estate business. Frank also
made a name for himself as a soldier in that part of the country.

As for Joe, he said, "I want to get back under the Union Jack,"
and consequently travelled back to western Canada. He ended up
in Lethbridge.

One night a roughly dressed, long-haired man from the range
appeared in the lobby of the town's main hotel with a bottle of thick,
black liquid. He passed it around and asked the loungers if they could
identify it.

Joe Grant, sitting back quietly observing the frontiers-man spoke up and said:

Let me smell that."

He was handed the bottle. He took a sniff and a quiver of excitement went through his nostrils.

"That is crude oil," he said. "Where did you get it?"

The frontiersman, who introduced himself as Kootenai Brown, did not take long in sizing up the big stranger as one knowing something about oil. He revealed that he had a little place near Waterton Lake and that some friends of his Indian wife, had led him to this seepage of oil on a nearby creek. The Indians and some whites had been gathering small quantitites of it and using it for medicinal and other purposes. The two talked a long time that night and at the end agreed, that they should obtain capital financing and Grant should go back to Ontario and bring a drill rig to the location and try drilling for the precious fluid. He convinced Brown that the venture would pay handsome dividends.

Grant headed back to Oil Springs, Ont., in 1891, and bought a spring pole tool outfit. He and Patrick Lineham began drilling a well near Waterton Lake Alberta, but the project ended in disaster. The rig caught fire and burned. There was not enough money to finance a new one. It was back to farming for Joe Grant.

He bought a flock of 1,000 sheep in Montana and brought them to a lease he secured on the Milk River Ridge. However, he was chased out of there by cattlemen who hated shepherds. They had a law that sheep could only be grazed near Medicine Hat. He was sold a ranch at Walsh by W.L. Nichol, a Medicine Hat butcher. Nichol was under pressure to sell because of a spot of difficulty he was having with his foreman, Louie Clark. He and Louie were in a partnership breaching the Scott Act, which made it illegal then to retail hard liquor in the West.

They were importing kegs of liquor in hogsheads of salt from Ontario. The salt was dumped over a cutbank and the whisky stored beneath hotbeds in the Nichol greenhouse. The hooch was hauled to The Hat under loads of produce — but the RNWMP never caught them.

Nichols and Clark had a falling out over division of profits and the best way Nichol could think of getting rid of his troublesome farmhand was to sell the ranch to Joe Grant.

To finance the purchase, Grant made a trip back to Oil Springs and raised capital among the Grants and Beattys, (one of whom was Edward, then a lawyer for the CPR in Montreal). He formed the Sarnia Ranching Company with 55,000 acres of leased and deeded land which, at the peak of its operation, supported 17,000 sheep.

When Grant heard of the Medicine Hat venture into gas exploitation a few years later, he let the ranch slide and went drilling. From 1901 on, he always seemed to be in trouble with municipal wells he had contracted.to drill. City engineer Morrison sought to ease the problems in 1909 by appointing Frosty Martin as consultant. However, Martin's appointment was never ratified by council.

In the drilling of a deeper well in 1909, Grant once again got into trouble. Frosty publicly questioned some of his methods. Such criticism by a loud-mouthed Yankee interloper touched off a row which raged for three years.

The omission of ratification of his appointment by council got Frosty fired. Grant continued drilling wells for the city until 1912, when he contracted what is known today as Alzheimer's Disease. He died in 1919 not being able to comprehend his contribution to Medicine Hat as a manufacturing city, because of its cheap gas supplies.

Frosty's spat with the Grant faction on council was to crop up again two years later when he and Tiny applied to the city for concessions in establishing an oil-tool-making foundry.

Although he was probably earning one of the highest salaries in Alberta at the time, he was not content to wear any man's collar. His main ambition was to go into business for himself — any kind would do so long as the profits from his labour were not reaped by somebody else.

The "tool plant" was the International Supply Company Ltd., a company which was to acquire seven strings of tools and take on contracts for 56 wells in Alberta and Saskatchewan, between 1912 and 1918.

At that time Alberta would do almost anything to attract industry. Medicine Hat had the edge by offering free gas; there was so much available that the gas lights on the streets and on the CPR station platform were never turned off. Other municipalities complained of the unfair gas giveaway practice. City officials defended the practice on the grounds that if the city didn't use the gas outside municipalities would tap the field and transport it away. Frosty Martin's statement that there was enough gas to last 100 years was further rationalization of that policy. He was right.

His request to the city was for a free three-acre site, 300,000 cubic feet of gas free of a day and no taxes for 10 years. Council put the proposition on a money bylaw for a vote of property owners at the 1912 civic elections Jan. 1. But the bylaw failed to carry the necessary two-thirds majority. Political enemies from the Grant faction had stirred up opposition.

However, Martin had some powerful friends on council, too, and at the inaugural meeting they brought forward a new bylaw with some changes, set another vote for Jan. 26 — and it carried. Tiny and Frosty were in business.

With Joe Grant on his sickbed, Martin and Phillips won a contract to drill nine civic wells from which the city retailed gas at 13¢ cents per 1,000.

Their shop was the first in Western Canada to make and repair drilling and fishing tools. They sold some of the first tools used in the new Turner Valley and Viking fields.

The company expanded until the start of the First World War and, like most companies in Medicine Hat's bustling industrial subdivision, they were forced to retrench as speculative capital for oil wildcatting dried up, or convert to the manufacture of artillery shells, for the British War Office.

A contract to Martin and Phillips was for machining 30,000 75-mm 18-pound shell casings. But they were unable to finance the installation of the required shell-making machinery. In 1915, their company was taken over by the better-financed Western Manufacturing and Supply Co. Limited of Calgary, and it completed the contract and others. Western Manufacturing resold their foundry to them after the war.

With the oil patch practically closed down and cash flow almost non-existent, they tried desperately to revive the business by acquiring the first Canadian agency for the Stinson tractor from Minneapolis in 1919. A four-wheel model sold for $2,000. Few of these were ever sold in the West, though, as they had poor dust seals. The company went bankrupt in 1920.

In 1921 Tiny and Frosty were forced into bankruptcy and a new company was organized but it, too, went bankrupt. The property was taken for taxes.

Frosty left town and headed back for the oil patch in the United States to recoup his fortunes. Tiny stayed on in the Alberta oil patch.

Neither Spud Martin nor Fred Phillips shared their parents' liking for the oil patch. However, they learned enough basics in the Medicine Hat plant, for Fred to go into the welding and ornamental iron works business in Calgary and Spud into the aircraft business in Long Beach, California.

Medicine Hat was always a city of innovation and tests. The public was amazed, for instance, when the CPR brought a passenger coach lighted by natural gas from wells in Medicine Hat, to the Dominion Exhibition in Calgary in 1908. It was hard for people to believe anything so volatile and so hard to confine and control could be utilized in this way.

The railroad had formerly used Pintsch gas, manufactured by distilling oil, for lighting the coaches. But it was too expensive. The gas was transported in steel flasks made to withstand 1,700 pounds per square inch. Later a method of transporting natural gas under only 150 pounds pressure was developed. The Pintsch incandescent mantle could be used alternately with gas.

Once it had perfected the system the railroad began using gas in trains 311 and 312 from Medicine Hat to Kootenay Landing, in flasks 35 feet long and eight inches in diameter. By the end of 1910, the experimental use of gas on these trains had proven so successful it was decided to extend use of gas to other division points.

The railroad ordered, from its German flask-making firm, two special cars for hauling 36 flasks in horizontal racks. By Christmas that year, the railway was filling a car of the gas transports every day at its Brooks gas well. Storage of the volatile gas had been perfected. The cars were hauled to all division points from Vancouver to Winnipeg. At some points it was used to mix with Pintsch gas; at others it replaced Pintsch, coal-oil and all forms of illumination.

Use of the gas was only discontinued, when the more-dependable belt generators for lighting came into use on the passenger cars.

The economy of Alberta is based on agriculture and oil — but not necessarily in that order. There has never been much accommo- dation between the two — just as there was never any love lost between cattlement and sheepmen, in the early days of the open range.

Chapter 11

J.D. McGregor's Prairie Development Scheme

One of the closer relationships among the pioneers of both industries was struck up between Tiny Phillips and James D. McGregor. McGregor was in on the ground floor of Western agriculture — dating from 1877 — 30 years before Tiny showed up in the West. Their paths crossed in Medicine Hat in 1906, when McGregor hired Phillips and Frosty Martin to drill those five wells for the Southern Alberta Land Company, of which he was manager. This was to fulfill a contractual obligation to supply irrigation for a land settlement project of such immensity, it still staggers the imaginations of Canadians.

In 1906, land in Western Canada was practically worthless as there was so much available with so few takers. The federal government Department of the Interior was selling it a $1 an acre, or renting it at two cents an acre for a maximum of two years. Thus, if the demand for settlement was pressing in any given area such leases could be readily broken and the land made available for pre-emption by settlers. However, if the leaseholders agreed to irrigation of some of the land, the government would extend the length of the lease. In a few cases "closed" grazing leases of larger size were granted for 21 years, to political friends of the government.

Had not McGregor been involved in the 380,000-acre SAL, there is no doubt the face of southern Alberta would have been vastly different than it is today. Beset by financial and irrigation difficulties, McGregor was never able to pull off much of what he had promised the government.

Tiny's scribbler makes frequent reference to the financially-complex operation in which McGregor was involved; and before that the family's travels after emigrating from Scotland in 1832. His grandfather settled first in Quebec. His father, David, came to Amherstburg, Ont., to farm and James Duncan was born there in 1860. Seventeen years later, the skinny young lad had his first look at Manitoba before the CPR came there.

John Wright Sifton, MLA St.
Clements. Photograph circa
1878. Photo: Manitoba
Archives.

Besides being a Scotsman, a Liberal and a Presbyterian — a combination that pushed back many frontiers in Canada — McGregor was a cattleman, both purebred and commercial. After rawhiding around the West in various cattle enterprises, the large McGregor family finally set up Glencarnock Farms with purebred Aberdeen Angus cattle at Brandon, Manitoba.

They sold beef cattle to John W. Sifton, one of the contractors on the new CPR coming through. The elder McGregor sold the first carload of cattle the now-famous Pat Burns ever bought.

John Sifton, an Irish immigrant, was in the oil business in Petrolia as a refiner and marketer following establishment of the first big play at Oil Springs, in 1858. He helped organize one of the world's first oil cartels in 1862: an agreement among producers to stabilize the price. He, himself, went broke in 1870 and headed for Brandon. Both sons, Clifford and Arthur, became lawyers and set up practices in Brandon in 1882.

McGregor became a lieutenant of Clifford Sifton in Liberal politics and helpted him get elected to both the provincial legislature and the House of Commons. In the latter he was appointed Minister of the Interior in 1898.

From that date onward, settlement of the West began at a fast pace. Sifton jettisoned a Conservative regulation that made it necessary for cabinet to sign every land transfer after it had passed through the civil service. He could not condone the bureaucratic mind which made the documents in a sale more important than the sale itself.

Although not a robust man, whatever Sifton chose to do he did it in a hard-driving, intense and furious way. He knew more about a situation than anyone else around him. He got things done fast. For instance, during the political campaign of 1896, he would come off the train at Brandon at 11 at night, get a few cronies together at his home, sit up all night, have them to breakfast and then, in the dead of winter, start out by sleigh to deliver speeches at Souris in the afternoon, Hartney at night and then drive across to Oak Lake to catch the train back again. All he needed was to pull the buffalo robe around him and sleep in the sleigh.

This kind of energy earned him the hatred of many opposition members. However, not having the CBC news department on his back with hourly accounts of his "treachery," he survived all the attacks but the Manitoba school question.

Sifton was the man on the spot to handle law and order, with the onset of the Yukon Gold Rush. He was appointed to show the flag for the Canadian government by walking halfway in to Dawson City, in the fall of 1897, with a group of administration officials he had appointed, to make sure law enforcement was well and truly put in place. One of the officials was J.D. McGregor, whose job it was to issue licences to miners to enable the government to collect a 10% royalty from them to finance the administration.

Because the administration was able to ride herd on the lawless element, (which mostly originated in the United States), the crooks organized protests — that got them nowhere — about the way Sifton's men handed out townsite leases and mining licences. Thomas Fawcett, the mining commissioner, came under the heaviest fire.

His sin was, that in the cause of chivalry, he did not require women to stand in line outside his office to file claims or do other business — but took them out of turn. To him a woman was a woman whether she came from Lousetown, the city's red light district, or from the home of a wealthy respected merchant.

His detractors criticized him for not singling out the whores for lesser attention than others.

No doubt he and his friend, McGregor, quietly chortled about this scandal after hours in the bar. He was able to assist McGregor in another matter later.

McGregor came out of the Yukon with a large-sized poke of gold, due to the commissioner's ruling that allowed him to stake a claim. He and Crown Attorney F.C. Wade staked claims on Monte Cristo Island because of insider knowledge. This drew wrathful newspaper editorials, as it was one of the richest claims on the Klondike River. But it was legal, as the government allowed its officials to stake as well as any other citizen, Fawcett ruled.

Most of McGregor's tour of duty saw square shooting and benevolence: such as the time he used a couple of year-old San Francisco newspapers to raise $10,000 towards establishment of a hospital. The miners were starved for news of the Outside. He therefore clipped out several hundred stories and offered them for sale. The miners paid big prices to buy a story from home. Due to his Scottish shrewdness, this gave them their hospital.

Tiny's scribbler: "McGregor told me he regarded his days in the Yukon as the most gratifying of his life, although they never exceeded the more spectacular days in Alberta which followed soon after he left the Yukon in 1901."

With the money he dug out of Monte Cristo Island, plus profits from Glencarnock Farms in Brandon, plus Sifton's generosity to a loyal friend in assigning government and irrigation leases, he was able to invest in his dream project in southern Alberta. He had come across the land while travelling across the Prairies, buying remount horses for Canadian troops in the Boer War, in South Africa.

He and some of his Yukon friends organized the Grand Forks Cattle Company and applied for a 47,000-acre grazing lease, near the confluence of the Bow and Belly Rivers in 1904. He also bought a lease of similar size, from Arthur and Alfred Edwin Hitchcock of Moose Jaw, in the same area and had Sifton declare the two as "closed." This meant that over the next 21 years, he had the right to buy 10% of the land for a homestead for $1 an acre.

McGregor didn't select the 9,000 acres of land he was entitled to buy in one block, but bought the choice quarter-sections. He set up a demonstration farm on a beautiful plateau high above the Bow River, a site he had selected for a townsite. He chose the name Ronalane, after Maj.-Gen. Sir Ronald Lane, president of the Southern Alberta Land Company.

Having done this, McGregor came under the influence of several persons described by Rudyard Kipling, as "flanneled fools." They managed to manipulate and upgrade McGregor's lease into 380,000 acres of irrigation lease, i.e., land that could be broken into smaller holdings and sold to settlers, at maybe $10 or $12 an acre, like the CPR was doing in its Eastern Irrigation and Western Irrigation Districts.

The money was easily raised for this work in England by the Canadian Agency, headed by Maj.-Gen. Guy St. Aubyn, a London stock broker. In the four years which ended in 1910, the agency raised the enormous amount of $50 million for Canadian settlement projects, mostly from 5,000 investors in the Manchester area of England.

It was McGregor's job to transfer his closed leases plus others to the Southern Alberta Land Company. He and the Hitchcocks took a profit of $957,000 from the deal.

The Tory opposition in the House of Commons raised hell about his wheeling and dealing. But Sifton was no longer there. However, Sir Wilfrid Laurier's Liberals beat back a motion of censure brought forward by M.S. McCarthy, the Conservative MP for Calgary. During this vote a Liberal named Henri Bourassa crossed party lines.

There are two ways of looking at the settlement of the West. Left to the inertia of the previous Conservative government and its civil service, the process suffered stagnation. Given a financial incentive under the new regime of Laurier, the promoting types brought in a flood of settlers within a few years. The fact they made a profit left them open to criticism in many quarters.

The Lethbridge News treated the middlemen in an unreasonable manner; it did not take into consideration that had not the middlemen been on the scene to bring the money from English investors, there would have been no assurance that sufficient capital would have flowed into this and other projects.

On the other hand, there is no gainsaying that the middlemen in this project put the settlers under a bigger burden than necessary, with profit-taking manoeuvres.

The News said if the government had sold the land directly to the people who proposed to irrigate it, all this rake-off would have been avoided and the settler would have obtained his land at cost price, with a reasonable profit to the men who, in good faith, invested their money. Or, if it was thought that the settlers could have afforded to pay those proposed prices, the sum of over $1 million which had been gathered in by the promotors and middlemen, would have gone to the Dominion treasurer.

Whether the rake-off had been taken from the Canadian taxpayer or from the Western farmer, it must be regarded as plunder, pure and simple, the News said.

It could see the necessity for the McGregors, Hitchcocks, Rosses, Murrays and other political speculators between the government and the genuine investor. It appeared to the News, however, that it was impossible under the present regime, to keep them out or to prevent them from getting their intermediate profits on other people's expenditures.

Back in the prairie solitude thousands of miles from the uproar in Ottawa, McGregor set out to inaugurate farming methods 100 years ahead of his time. He used dryland irrigation methods. He had a 30-cow dairy farm and a hog enterprise. He showed that under irrigation, every king of vegetable from sweet corn to watermelons could be grown. Indeed, he shipped some of these to market by CP Express. But the market couldn't use the abundance. He planted a million trees as windbreaks amid the laughter of his fellow ranchers.

Fruit trees were grown but hail ruined them. Crops were non-existent some years because of drought or hail. The winter of 1906-7 was cruelly cold. He was successful in showing alfalfa could increase the tilth of the soil. He had bees for pollination. Sugar beets and a sugar factory were a possibility.

McGregor was a regular commuter between Brandon and Medicine Hat; and to Great Britain to report to SAL directors in London and buy Angus cattle from Scotland for breeding.

When he wasn't commuting, he was engaged in organizing two subsidiary companies in conjunction with Arthur M. Grenfell of the Canadian Agency. One was the Canadian Wheat Lands Limited, which comprised 100,000 acres in the Suffield-Bowell area north of Medicine Hat, which it bought or optioned from SAL. SAL had an agreement to build an irrigation system and supply water to the wheat lands. This was to be accomplished by extending the SAL's main canal across the Bow River at Ronalane, by a siphon or pipeline. Until water arrived it was decided to break some of the land for wheat growing. This was carried out by hundreds of men, mules, horses and oxen and became one of Canada's largest farming enterprises.

The second subsidiary set up was the Alberta Land Company. This comprised 67,674 acres acquired by this company, from Francis Percival Aylwin and 20,000 acres of land from the Hudson's Bay Company. The SAL had a contract to build irrigation works and supply water to irrigate this land. The tract was east of Lake McGregor and west of the Bow River. Bow City was its "capital." At the time of his deal some of the opposition members in the House of Commons became furious and kicked up a great political storm. McGregor and Grenfell of the Canadian Agency were forced to tread lightly in the floating of this company.

The year 1912 saw two events transpire which, with one stroke, equalled McGregor's business career quite conclusively and set the stage for a livestock show ring exploit, which has never been equalled. In the first instance, he was relieved of his job as manager of the Southern Alberta Land Company by the English directors. In the second, two of his black Angus steers won the grand championships at the International Livestock Exposition in Chicago in two successive years.

Plans for the Southern Alberta Land Company irrigation system had been completed and construction of the main irrigation canal, or "big ditch", began in 1909, with completion date set for the fall of 1912. One of the most difficult projects was the throwing of the dam, or weir, across the Bow River near what is now Carseland, to divert water down the big ditch.

Now, the Bow is no river for even the best engineers to trifle with at the best of times. While it looks innocent in summer, running peacefully and silkily through a channel cut 300 feet deep through the foothills and prairies, it is noted for its tendency to scour structures thrown across it — and there are many quicksand traps. In the break-up it runs swift, cold and ful of ice ready to batter anything in its path.

The fury of the spring freshet vented itself upon the SAL dam in late May, 1912. The intake collapsed as the result of water washing out a large section. Other troubles were experienced during the heavy mountain run off in July and it became apparent, it could not be repaired for the grand official opening set for Sept. 7.

The official opening ceremonies were planned at Gleichen as one of the most glamorous and glittering occasions in the history of Alberta.

The Duke of Connaught, Canada's governor-general, was invited to do the honours and he accepted. Two reasons prompted his acceptance:

1. The invitation was extended by the president of the Southern Alberta Land Company, Sir Ronald Lane. The duke had formerly been Sir Ronald's commanding officer in the British forces.

2. The opening was planned to coincide with the duke's appearance at the first Calgary Stampede Sept. 5, 1912. These official functions were only two of the many the duke was called upon to participate in during a tour of the Canadian West, by special train in company with his wife and his daughter, Princess Patricia.

The opening ceremonies in Gleichen were no problem. The townspeople and CPR went all out to accommodate a guest list, that included about half of Burke's Peerage, it seemed. But McGregor determined none of the directors were going to see the wreckage of the Carseland dam.

He led a tour of 30 open-top cars; to take the duke and investors 28 miles to the dam in advance of the dinner. But there had been heavy rains and the wagon roads were mudholes. In attempting to circumvent the muddy road, McGregor somehow got "lost" and drove in circles for eight hours on the bald-headed, trackless prairie without finding the wreckage of the dam.

Unfortunately for him, his cover was blown by a flat tire on the car at the tailend of the procession. The car was occupied by Lawrence

Jones, a young English barrister travelling with Sir Ronald Lane. The flat took the driver a long time to repair and when he finished the rest were out of sight. He took Jones and a young Canadian reporter directly to the damsite.

When Jones came back he reported what had actually happened to Lane. Lane immediately turned purple. A look of panic was detected behind McGregor's thick-lensed spectacles. Lane sacked him on the spot.

The embarrassed Britishers managed to keep a stiff upper lip and to cover up the story, so it never showed up in print in Canada.

Big Mac's position as general manager was filed for a time by Alex C. Newton, brother of Capt. D.C. Newton, Canadian Agency representative in Montreal. D.W. Hays of Denver, Colo., an irrigation engineer with the United States Reclamation Service, replaced A.M. Grace as chief engineer.

Later, the true story was told over and over by company personnel around the Elks Club and the Cypress Club and Tiny and Frosty heard snatches of it. Nobody in Canada held his desperate cover-up against McGregor. His relatives continued to work at SAL farming enterprises until SAL folded in 1914, because of the outbreak of the First World War, Aug. 5 and the infusion of British funds was suspended.

The outbreak of the war set Alberta agriculture, then the province's biggest expansion industry, back more than anything in its history. The British and their millions never came back after the war. True, they came in some numbers, but were supplanted by a huge migration from the United States, which included Hutterites.

The historians have never agreed on where the agricultural potential would have gone if those irrigation systems and other plans organized by them would have remained solvent.

McGregor's contribution and his dedication to agriculture were never in question. He was one of the brainstrust behind the formation of the 4-H clubs of Canada, as president of the Brandon Fair in 1913.

His contribution to livestock was recognized in the U.S. when his portrait was hung in the Saddle and Sirloin Club, at the International Livestock Exposition in Chicago, in 1928. That same year he sold his entire Angus breeding herd to Australia.

He did equally well in Canada, as his portrait was hung in the Canadian Agricultural Hall of Fame at the Royal Agricultural Winter Fair in Toronto, in 1961, the first year of the awards.

In 1929 at the age of 69, he was appointed lieutenant-governor of Manitoba on recommendation of the Mackenzie King government.

He died of pneumonia at age 75 while in office, still a strong, husky man.

He came out West when the country was young and rangy and never curried below the knees. As Tiny Phillips wrote in his scribbler in 1963;

"Progress won't catch up to him for another 50 years."

Chapter 12

The Alamo Hotel at Suffield

A*round Sylvan Lake, Alberta,* they still talk with amazement about the Chicago tourist who walked off in triumph one summer day, with an unusual curio from the town hotel: an old, small, square flush toilet.

U.S. tourists have raided Canada for every conceivable kind of historical keepsake and have succeeded in doing it without criticism, as Canadians have not been quick enough to recognize their value as museum pieces.

No less strange than this tourist's interest in waste disposal history, is the history of the hotel itself.

It was first erected in Suffied, 20 miles northwest of Medicine Hat in 1910, by three U.S. citizens, Tiny Phillips and Frosty Martin and A.M. Grace, the first chief engineer of the Southern Alberta Land Company. They had a finger in the early devleopment of Suffield, a village with a strange and fascinating history.

In 1909, the SAL had selected this CPR siding named after the fifth Baron of Suffield, one of the railway's financial backers, as a future townsite and headquarters for all its holdings east of Ronalane. Suffield became, in effect, headquarters for the Canadian Wheat Lands Limited.

The head office for both CWL and SAL was a large, red brick block. Directors of both companies in far-off London had visions of Suffield becoming the centre of a vast, desert metropolis, which they proposed to make bloom by the installation of a giant irrigation system. As a matter of fact, $11 million was spent by the company in an effort to make this happen.

The SAL published a prospectus for the town and distributed it among its shareholders and those of the various associated companies. The company induced some of their employees to invest in lots. Some later discovered they had deeds to lots, even without their knowledge. The promotion caught public fancy and it soon became one of the fastest-growing towns in the West.

The Alama Hotel was moved from Suffield to Sylvan Lake. The 40-foot stand-up bar, was considered one of the finest in Canada.

Many important people bought lots, ranging from Mack Higdon, a construction contractor on SAL, to Lady Agatha Lilian Baroness Hindlip, wife of Charles Allsop, Baron Hindlip of Worcester, who paid $300 each for two lots. She made the purchase Sept. 22, 1911, through her solicitors, Oldfield, Kirby and Gardner of Winnipeg. The purchase assured that the nearby lake resort of Agatha was named after her. That townsite never reached development. Lord Hindlip was a director of CWL and made frequent visits to Suffield, to inspect his large investment.

Suffield also became headquarters for a number of contractors working on irrigation ditches in the area. Altogether there were 500 workers employed in the area, while the townsite was being promoted from 1909 to 1914.

In 1909, things were really booming when $50,000 worth of town lots were sold. Martin, Phillips and Grace decided another hotel was needed. In a civilized country one couldn't ask the likes of Lord Hindlip, Arthur M. Grenfell or Francis Percival Aylwin, a civil servant from Ottawa, to bunk in at either of the other two hostelries.

One was the Albion, which was operated in an indifferent manner in the same building as the J.D. McGregor hardware store, by Dan Doyle, a district farmer. Mine Host Doyle, was always hard-pressed for cash. SAL accountants were continually receiving promises-to-pay the rent from him.

In 1917, he promised faithfully they would get their money when a quantity of wheat he was holding, reached $2 a bushel. When this happened they held him to his promise; they were right in the lobby the minute the announcement came.

Business was bad during and after the war and old Dan spent a great deal of his time seeking rent reductions — even up to the time of his death in 1921. After a series of lessees, the SAL decided to sell the hotel. It was bought in 1923 by Reeve F.J. Hankel for $700. The building originally cost $1,500. It was worth only $300 when it was sold.

The third hotel was the Temperance. It lived up to its name. The thirsty traveller, like Lord Hindlip, could not obtain a drink there before or after Prohibition. So it was up to Martin, Phillips and Grace to jump into the breach.

The hotel was the Alamo, named by Martin. He had spent eight years in the drilling business prior to coming to Canada and the Alamo was a favorite retreat on visits to Texas. The lobby contained a number of pictures of that historic spot.

A reporter for the Medicine Hat News gave a more complete report on the Alamo Hotel than Tiny's scribbler. Standing in awe of the only three-storey structure for miles on the raw,open, short-grass prairie, the reporter wrote Oct. 20, 1910:

"The most beautiful hotel alongside the CPR from Winnipeg to Calgary, stands on the prairie within a stone's throw of one of the biggest gas wells in the Medicine Hat district in what promises to be, in the near future, the city of Suffield.

Seen from a flying CPR express, the big hotel with lights blazing is not unpromising of the reknown that is about to come.

It is a 32-room hostelry and has been erected at a cost of approximately $30,000 by Messrs. W.R. Martin, superintendent of CPR oil and gas exploration; A.M. Grace, chief engineer of the Southern Alberta Land Company, and A.P. Phillips, oil and gas driller.

The fact that the town is in the making, has not deterred these men from equipping their jewel box of a hotel with every conceivable modern attachment, for the safety and comfort of the guests and the interior is particularly beautiful.

Martin, to whom the credit of designing is due, has been at endless pains to demonstrate the possibilities of severe lines and solf colourings.

The furnishings and fittings throughout are of the plainest richness imaginable and the effect is one which will be striven for by innumerable copyists.

From the wide gallery running across the front of the building and open to the breezes of the prairies, handsome doors open into a rotunda of excellent proportions. The rough finished walls, kalsomimed in soft brown tints and burlapped in a darker shade, the weathered oak furniture, the plate glass windows and hard maple floors are a model of what may be accomplished by carefully adapted mission variations.

Open from it at the right is the bar room suggestive of the eastern forests with its rich deep green walls and dull mission base of utterly plain lines after Martin's own pet idea. The back bar is adapted from the model of a buffet and filled with cut glass of rarely beautiful patterns. Above the unobtrusive but elegant mirrors small windows of art glass admit the light in subdued colours.

The dining room, decorated in Turkish red, competes a trinomial of soft colours which, for artistic effect, could not have been excelled. In the dining room the furniture is again mission oak in soft harmony with burlap and paler red of the upper wall.

Beautifully plain flatware and the Alamo stamp are distinctive features of the appointments.

The second floor accommodates 17 apartments exactly similar in dimensions and furnishings and two suites and a drawing room. Soft green is the prevailing colour and lines are severly plain with bush brass beds, mahogany furniture, Brussels rugs and ecru curtains and supplied with hot and cold water.

The drawing room is decorated in reddish buff tone on walls and there is an Axminister rug on the floor. Mission furniture is used.

The long corridors are carpeted with dark green Wilton. The single rooms on both the second and third floors have Brussels rugs.

Iron beds and oak furniture are used throughout. The third floor is decorated with red and blue.

The basement accommodates an ample refrigerator, vegetable cellar, wine cellar, steam heating plant and a big well lighted sample room.

In the commodious kitchen and pantry all the latest conveniences are arranged.

The hotel will be lighted with natural gas and has a private water supply from a 230-foot well in sandstone strata. The water is pumped to a large tank on the thrid floor and is distributed to various apartments and toilet rooms. The tank capacity is 100 barrels.

An excellent system of fire protection has been put in with fire alarms on each floor. Electric annunciators are placed in each room.

The stairway is the centre of the building and serves as a light and air shaft.

The severity of the lines and the entire absence of decoration is relieved by the first-class quality of the material used everywhere, even in such minute details as net curtains, holland blinds, felt mattresses and eiderdown comforters.

The manager is Leo Hughes. Miss Cooperman has charge of the culinary department.

The hotel has been named distinctively in keeping with its appearance. The lobby will be adorned with a number of distinctive cuts of the historic "Alamo" in Texas, which was a favorite retreat of Martin during his eight-year sojourn south of the Rio Grande before coming to Canada.

It has not yet been formally opened but the Ladies Aid recently held a dance with 100 present. Proceeds will be used to furnish a school being built by public subscription.

Music was furnished by Messrs. Field, Phillips and Green.

The Alamo Hotel in Suffield became more or less the social centre of the booming village. Mrs. Jack Orr, who has been in Suffield since 1914, recalls that a number of wedding receptions were held there. When her sister, Marcella Nowicki, was married to Albert Lund, her father rented a whole floor of the Alamo. Everyone around town knew her father as "Old Joe" Nowicki. He worked as a section foreman on the CPR. Since the CPR owned vast tracts of land on each side of the right-of-way, it was easy for the section men in those days to run large numbers of horses on company land. Many of the horses raised by "Old Joe", saw service building the land company's ditch.

Another attraction was the 40-foot stand-up bar, one of the finest in the country.

Good food was always the mainstay of the Alamo. Travellers were attracted for this reason, especially on Sunday when people would drive out for dinner from Medicine Hat. One of the specialities of the house, (in season), was oysters. Since ordinary meals were 15 to 35 cents, the oyster suppers at $1 were lavish affairs. It must be remembered, this typically Amerian seafood was a rare treat in the middle of the sparsely settled prairie. Zulah Phillips was in charge of the kitchen.

One couldn't get a room without a reservation, in the hotel, during the years 1910-1912.

In later years, people said, there was a noticeable swaying when a high wind blew off the prairie — and there are some stiff winds in those wide open spaces in the dry country. However, guests of the day were little incommoded by this small inconvenience. Quite possibly the pink lap siding provided prestige enough to outweigh any inconvenience.

The place made money, and no doubt the original investment was quickly paid off. With capital funds coming in at a fast rate, it was fairly easy for anyone of any affluence to negotiate a loan to go into such a business.

A double blow hit the hotel. At the coming of the First World War, the supply of English capital came to an end and the land company operations were greatly reduced. Then in 1915, the supply of booze dried up with the arrival of Prohibition. The hotel was sold as there was not enough trade to support it. Mrs. George Ferguson, managed it for a time for Tiny Phillips. The last owner was Mrs. William George.

The once-proud hotel stood empty a number of years. Then in 1926, the hotel on the main corner of Sylvan Lake burned down. Calgary Brewing and Malting Company needed a new hotel quickly. It acquired the Alamo Hotel in Suffield and moved it to Sylvan Lake the next year and had it re-erected on a lot, on the opposite corner of the razed structure.

Jim Stevenson, a Calgary architect, was called in to supervise the job of moving the building and re-erecting it. This proved to be a more difficult job than at first expected. The owners assumed the building would be perfectly preserved by the dry air of the prairies. This was not so. There were a great many sills affected by dry rot.

In 1927, Sylvan Lake had not attained its present-day popularity. Its undeveloped shoreline was described as a "slough." The village picked up the nickname, Slimy Lake. There was a shortage of drinking and washing water. It was for this reason the architect had extra-small wash bowls installed in the rooms: to conserve the water supply.

His friends at the lake dubbed these installations, "Jim Stevenson's Piss Pots."

And, of course, it was Stevenson who drew the specifications for the smaller-than-normal toilets, whose discovery made the American collector a happy man.

The only vestige of the hotel in Suffield now is a concrete base, where an engine sat outside the hotel. It was used to pump water to a 100-gallon tank on the third floor, for supplying hot water for the guests and for fire protection.

The building of the Alamo Hotel was only an incidental part of the real business, that brought Martin and Phillips to town. They were hired by SAL to drill a gas well to supply light and heat for the town. The well still performs today.

Prior to that, they drilled a gas well to replace a gasoline engine that kept the CPR water tank at Suffield filled. The engine was located 11 miles away on the South Saskatchewan River, but the railway was having a problem. The hot, dry weather shrank the wooden barrels in which the gasoline was transported and they leaked badly. Some of the 45-gallon barrels arrived with only four or five gallons left in them.

The water was pumped via pipeline to a dugout four miles away and ran by gravity from there, to the Suffield water tank. This system worked until 1945.

Social services in the town were minimal — even at the peak population of 200. The Anglican Church of Canada bought a shack for $50 from SAL for its services. The Methodists rented a room in the school, which was two shacks thrown together.

None of the grocery stores ever made money.

The Bank of Montreal built a branch in a small building in 1910, which elicited a memo in Tiny's scribbler:

It had a sign in the window which was a source of wonderment to us Americans: "Assets, $14 million."

Few of the privately owned banks in the U.S., could boast of such large reserves. The Americans were not familiar with Canada's system of chartered banks, in which the assets of the whole system across the nation were totalled and advertised at each of the branches.

Business was done in a relatively informal manner. It was "next year" country and, as was the custom, people operated on credit with the merchants and paid off all debts once or twice a year — if they had the money.

The bar at the Alamo was a great forum for discussion of CWL affairs by the company personnel. None agreed too much with the eagerness of George G. Anderson, an irrigation engineer who had come from the U.S. via the Alberta Railway and Irrigation Company in Lethbridge, to get the whole 64,000 acres broken up and seeded to wheat to make money immediately for the company. J.D. McGregor advised against this rash step. He wanted to break up only 10,000 acres at a time and get them producing, as larger acreages would be too unwieldy to handle. Having broken the smaller acreages, they would, in turn, be broken down into smaller farms with some irrigated acres and sold to settlers. These would be possible to diversify widely — with a greater chance of a profit.

The agreement was drawn up between SAL and CWL by R.B. Bennett, a Calgary lawyer, who later became prime minister of Canada during the "Dirty '30s."

Although the agricultural know-how of McGregor was good, only minimal planning was done and no detailed examination of the soil quality throughout the tract was carried out in the field. The tracts to be irrigated were shown on a map in the office. It was only years later the company shareholders discovered the whole tract they bought was the poorest, roughest and least suited land in the whole province for irrigating.

W.H. Fairfield, superintendent of the Lethbridge Research Station, was offered the job of farm manager at $5,000 a year. He looked things over, and walked away from that princely salary. He didn't like what he saw. Company officials were too optimistic in their development plans.

James Murray, a graduate of the Ontario Agricultural College at Guelph and superintendent of the Brandon Research Station, was hired. He later became principal of Olds Agricultural School. He set up operations at 15 strategically located camps.

Initial attempts at plowing were made with 75 mules bought in St. Louis, Mo., as they could get along with less water than horses. Later, 100 oxen were bought from a Doukhobor settlement at Canora, Sask., and 30 Doukhobor teamsters came to drive them. They were used a couple of seasons then sold to the meat-packing firm of Gordon, Ironside and Fares at Moose Jaw.

Many yarns were told about the oxen and their drivers. When the hot days of July came, the foreman told the boys to take it easy.

One evening he asked one of the Doukhobor drivers: "Well, how did you make out today, Joe?"

"Fine, fine, boss, I made two rounds this morning and one this afternoon and I didn't hurry a bit."

Each round was two miles.

There were also eight tractors — three of them being Avery steamers.

One of the young engineers, (an engineer, fireman and plowman comprised a crew), was O.S. Longman, a Manitoba Agricultural College student from Brandon, who later became deputy Minister of Agriculture for Alberta.

Each steamer travelled 18 miles a day, pulling 10 or 12 Cockshutt plows which broke 56 acres. The practice at the time was to break the land in spring or summer, backset it in the fall and plant it the following spring. Backsetting was plowing the opposite way and pulling a set of harrows behind the plow. This is the way much of the Canadian prairies were broken.

Longman did some backsetting in the fall of 1912. He had learned enough about soils to realize, with horror, most of this land should never have been put to the plow. The sun had baked the soil hard; so hard the tractors could only pull three plows. Once that thin topsoil was distrubed, the land was left open to the elements and much began to blow.

Longman got off a CPR passenger train one Sunday morning in the spring of 1912. Being of a modest nature, he didn't rush right over to Murray's house with the expectation of being greeted with open arms. Instead, he did as most farmers do and "went out to the barn" to have a look around.

The barn was the biggest he had ever seen — with stalls for 225 horses and mules. The thing that struck him most, was the natural gas-driven pump used to pump water for the animals. The gas came in under pressure from the town well that Tiny and Frosty had drilled.

Between the line and the engine was a rubber bag or balloon. The idea of the balloon was to keep the pressure uniform as the gas went into the carburetor.

The horse, mule and oxen camps left a great deal to be desired. The bunk shacks were rudimentary and dirty and occupied by rough men whose idea of cleanliness, was to sweep the dirt into the corners. The Swedes were not very circumspect about where they expectorated their cuds of snuff. There was usually plenty of food but the cook was invariably the last man hired the day before. There was a high labour turnover. Jock McCulloch, who worked there a short time and later became editor of the Toronto Star Weekly, wrote:

"We hated the dull dogs and surroundings in which we had to work and we soon left." The ambitions of any young fellow who knew anything about plowing, was to get on the crew of one of the tractors. There was something romantic and fascinating, about seeiong these big engines making a ribbon a dozen plow widths and a mile long. Almost everyone was young and full of optimism and had an appetite like a horse.

It was thrilling to operate those big engines. But sometimes, with bad water, slack coal, leaky flues and foaming boilers, there was grief and worry, too.

The tractors created problems for the farmers later as they were the means of destruction for much of the semi-arid desert land in this part of the Palliser Triangle. In fact, some of the land was doomed forever.

Some wheat was actually grown and harvested in 1912 on the CWL, but not enough to clear expenses. Things looked good for 1913, until hot prairie winds in June dried out the crop and it wasn't even worth sending out the binders at havest time. None was harvested in 1914. The company directors knew by then they were in big trouble; the SAL had never delivered any water. Farm manager Murray was told to try to salvage what he could of the operation in 1915, as the commencement of the war had decimated the staff.

Nature has a funny way of pushing Western farmers to the wall for several years, then bouncing them back with bumper crops. The trick is to be able to hang on through the dry periods.

The phenomenon happened in 1915, when 16 inches of rain fell in the growing season, compared to only 15 the whole year previous. The desperate need of wheat by Britain saw the price advance towards the $2 a bushel mark.

Murray's solution was to rent the cultivated land to Medicine Hat contractors, whose machinery had been idled by the shut-down of construction on CWL. They planted wheat and they hit the jackpot in 1915. It grew shoulder-high.

The operation was repeated in 1916 on a smaller scale. Those two crops would have probably recouped CWL fortunes — but it was too late for that. CWL went into bankruptcy.

Jack McLane, agent for the receiver, sold off the lands eventually in 1924-7 at $1 an acre.

Along with an amalgamation of SAL with CWL and other subsidiaries in 1917, the drought returned. There was now no commitment for SAL to supply CWL with irrigation works. Operations were reduced and the once-cultivated fields allowed to grow up in weeds. Eventually, some of the native prairie grasses grew back but not as abundantly as before.

In 1920, some Montana sheepmen took out a three-year grazing lease and brought in 100,000 sheep. At the end of the lease, prairie fires and sheep had pretty well denuded the soil.

The onslaught of the Second World War saw a revival of Suffield, when the British War Office persuaded the Alberta government to expropriate 1,000 square miles of short-grass prairie, (half the size of Prince Edward Island), as a top-secret research and development station for chemical and germ warfare. Several hundred farmers were displaced.

The model town of Ralston on the base was developed. Suffield experienced a small come-back when Ralston residents bought Suffield lots, to make them eligible to collect Medicare payments.

The Suffield area has never made a comeback in agriculture, although several attempts have been made to revive the CWL irrigation scheme. It has, however, made a big come-back in the oil patch, as deeper drilling extending into the 1980s proved up many productive gas wells.

Chapter 13

To Wetaskiwin and Camrose

W*hen Eugene Coste* brought his American oil drillers extraordinaire, Tiny Phillips and Frosty Martin, to Medicine Hat, they could pretty well write their own ticket in a brawling new industry. However, by the time they had set up their International Supply Company with seven strings of standard tools in 1912, their abilities were challenged by some other new drilling companies. They first ran into stiff competition during the City of Wetaskiwin's adventure into natural gas. When they arrived there in 1913, they found Joe Grant, their old nemesis from Medicine Hat, already on the scene. In 1910, council had let a contract to Grant to drill a gas well to supply a cheaper fuel than coal, from the Battle River mines to power its electric light plant. The contract called for him to drill to 2,000 feet, where the gas supposedly was. It soon became apparent his pole tool rig was not up to drilling to that depth. He was losing money at the $7.50 a foot specified in the contract. He pecked away at the unyielding rock for three summers, before it dawned upon the citizens he wasn't going to be successful.

Grant was asked to attend a council meeting in January, 1913. He was by then a very sick man. When council cancelled his contract it was the end of an active life for poor old Joe.

Tiny and Frosty knew of this situation and were sitting on the sidelines, waiting for the nod from council to move in with their better tools. However, they were beaten out by Northwest Drilling Company of Calgary. The principals of the company, organized in 1911, were T. Max Fyshe and Edward N. Martin of a firm of engineers and general contractors and James Watson Kelly of Victoria, B.C. The corporate structure was shaky and there were frequent games of musical chairs among the personnel.

In November, 1913, Northwest Drilling proclaimed itself, in an ad in the Natural Gas and Oil Record of Calgary, as "probably the biggest drilling company in Canada today."

This prompted the International Supply Company to buy advertising space the next issue, denouncing that claim and pointing out it had drilled at least 10,000 more feet of hole than Northwest Drilling.

Northwest assumed the Wetaskiwin contract in May and allowed council $3,500 on the work already done by Grant. Northwest hit a gas "vein," it was reported by V.C. French, editor of the Wetaskiwin Times. Alas, it was not pay sand and council decided to raise $6,000 to deepen the well by a debenture bylaw.

In 1913, investment capital was not as readily raised as it is today. There were no investment brokers competing for debenture business. In fact, it was sometimes necessary for municipalities to despatch emissaries to The City in London, England, to find investors for muncipal issues, thus taking many months to raise the funds.

In the case of Wetaskiwin, the council decided to seek a $2,500 loan from the Bank of Montreal to tide it over until the debenture arrived. The note was backed by $100 pledges from 30 businessmen. However, the bankers suffered from stupidity and remoteness from reality and refused the loan. They apparently had little faith in the credit ratings of some of the businessmen who had signed pledges. The truth was more likely, that they reacted with the reserve of bankers everywhere against new and unproven industries.

Councillors were even more maddened by twitting from C.A. Heyden of the Calgary News-Telegram, who said: "This contretemps could have been avoided if the merchants had banded together and contributed $2,500 . . . . However, when the debentures find a market, it will be a case of all's well that ends well but, if not, we'll see the end of the gas well."

Damned smart alec!

The bank's mulish refusal didn't stop drilling; it merely slowed it down. Unfortunately, Northwest ran into trouble and the well proved to be semi-useless.

The citizens spent another cold winter without gas and by March, they were in a mood to spend money to drill two more wells.

To play it safe, they consulted R.S. Winter, CPR gas inspector of Medicine Hat. He gave the councillors some good technical advice on the calling of tenders which, it turned out later, only International Supply Company of Medicine Hat could meet. Tenders from Northwest Drilling and a California company were rejected, even though the Californians had promised to bring in one of the new rotary rigs. Had this drill come into the scene and drilled deeper to where the pay sand really was, Wetaskiwin would have become the centre of the oil patch in Alberta. The ante for this project was $31,000.

Tiny fumed in his scribbler that he and Frosty were not able to get their rig on the ground until August, because of slow freight delivery schedules of the CPR and because of the pressure of drilling other wells at Turner Valley, Olds and at a small town called Viking.

The first of a number of small disagreements with council started, when Frosty made the logistical error of asking it for $2,000 under the contract, before the rig was even on the site at the fairgrounds.

Just to make things interesting, Watt and Watt organized Wetaskiwin Petroleum Ltd. They placed before the first council meeting in July, a proposition to take over the drilling of both gas wells with a view to going to 3,000 feet to obtain oil. They wanted the city to contribute $15,000. They would finance drilling and if they struck oil they would keep it and give the city any gas struck. For the oil they took, they would pay a royalty of 10%.

Although there was gambling blood in the city coucil's veins, this proposition appeared a little too rich for the aldermen. After giving it some serious consideration, they quietly tabled the matter and let it drop.

In September, 1913, International Supply Company brought in No. 2 with indifferent production, was engaged in trying to clean out No. 1 and spudded in on No. 3. However, by December, the $31,000 had almost been used up and there was not enough to continue drilling No. 3.

Little drilling and a lot of bickering over contract payments were carried out in 1914. This situation developed into continuing political warfare. But by Christmas, a truce had been declared and the ratepayers voted to put out another $30,000 on a money bylaw.

Frosty Martin was running a little scared at this time, because the onset of the First World War had brought a quick end to the Turner Valley oil boom and most Canadians were doggedly pursuing the war effort. He therefore appeared before council, put the money bylaw to a vote and offered to take the debenture from the city at 95 cents on the $1, to ensure that International Supply Company got the contract. This would enable him to keep a drill crew at work without interruption. The ratepayers voted "yes."

Drilling continued until July, 1915, when the money ran out and work proceeded on a day-to-day basis at $1,680 a day.

On Aug. 1, work on the well was suddenly halted. A secret meeting of council was convened to consider action. Editor French had the door slammed in his face and was told his presence wasn't required at the meeting. He reacted by never mentioning the gas well problem in The Times again.

In January, 1916, it was decided to halt drilling and torpedo the well. This brought in an indifferent flow.

Frosty and Tiny quietly drifted away in mid-1916. The wells produced enough to supply the power plant and the Driard Hotel until 1948.

A gas well for Camrose, was another contract won by the fledgling Internationl Supply Company of Medicine Hat. The city, 25 miles southeast of Wetaskiwin, decided to go a different route for drilling: letting private enterprise take on the project.

This came about through the efforts of Francois Adam. He was a Belgian civil engineer who suffered a personal tragedy and came to Canada in 1883, to "get away from it all." After a number of years, he acquired a ranch at Duhamel where, in time, he built up an open range herd of 8,000 head of cattle — a not unusual number for some of the large operators of the day. With the coming of the Canadian Northern Railway, he reduced his holdings by selling homestead quarter-sections to settlers.

With the monies gained, he became a community leader, giving generously to public projects. When it was decided to drill for gas in Camrose, he was asked to head the company, Camrose Natural Gas Company, as his engineering experience would be valuable. He gathered up $24,000 by May, 1913, and a month later Northwest Drilling Company was asked to drill. However, Northwest never got the job. Frosty Martin slipped in with a late tender and his company was given the nod. While this procedure was somewhat unorthodox, nobody could do anything about it as the company was a private company and had the right to handle tenders the way it chose. There was no question of public tendering, nor the ethics of accepting a tender after the deadline.

There was a delay in site location because of an argument by the town fathers. Thus, it wasn't until Aug. 14, that four carloads of drilling machinery left Medicine Hat for Camrose.

By the time Tiny and Frosty began delivering the machinery the dispute had not been resolved — and wasn't until Sept. 18.

While cooling his heels, Frosty made several trips to Camrose to make himself known. George P. Smith, publisher of The Camrose Canadian, introduced Frosty to his readers in several long articles. One revealed he had been in the drilling business 25 years all over North America, South America, 38 states of the U.S., four provinces of Canada and Mexico.

A small flow of gas was brought in by Christmas Day. But by that time the gas company's contract had run out. At a public meeting between Christmas and New Year's, 1914, the ratepayers decided to leave the well as it was, (rather than drill deeper to better pay sand), and operate the power house with it.

Some time between then and May, an attempt was made to drill deeper. This was successful and gave the town a first-class water well which lasted many years.

The tools were removed and taken to Viking No. 1 well — a more exciting gas play and a re-run of the Bow Island field.

Chapter *14*

Difficulties at Viking

In Tiny's scribbler for 1914 there are frequent references to the Ad Club. It was a promotional venture, pushed by Mayor W.J. McNamara of Edmonton and ramrodded by W.J. Magrath, to counteract all the public adulation rival Calgary was receiving from the Turner Valley oil boom. It was a subsidiary of the Edmonton Industrial Association, a super-chamber of commerce, with 35 member municipalities around Edmonton. A forerunner of the nationwide Advertising and Sales Clubs, it published a pamphlet giving descriptions of agricultural and industrial opportunities. Although well-conceived and executed, the promotion proved abortive as Canada went to war that year and for the next four years the efforts of most people were spent promoting the war effort.

However, before the Ad Club gave up the ghost, it took a flyer into the gas business to give Edmontonians cheap heating fuel. The events leading up to this adventure were put in perspective by John W. Johnston, who edited The Viking News for the first five months of 1914. Then he left to "rusticate" on a homestead near Fort Saskatchewan.

While Johnston wielded the editor's pen, he proved to be a whimsical writer, never taking people too seriously but, fortunately for later researchers, recorded local happenings with an historical sense for detail. This waggish story appeared Jan. 29, 1914:

"Gas experts have detected gas at Bruce, 15 miles northwest of here. When word got to Mayor W.J. McNamara of Edmonton, who was sitting with his head buried deep in a desk full of knotty problems, he sniffed the air and said: 'I smell gas.' He straightaway dismissed his stenographer, slammed down his desk cover and ran out of the building, without hat or coat into 30 below zero weather and in a few quick breaths told W.J. Magrath of the Ad Club and the Edmonton Industrial Association all about it."

The gas experts were F.G. Clapp and his assistant L.G. Huntley of Pittsburgh, Pa., who had prepared an assessment of the Canadian oil patch resources for the federal mines department. After delivering the report they took off for China and Mexico respectively.

They also did a special $4,000 study for the Ad Club, which stated gas prospects were most promising in the Viking area. They recommended the drilling of three wildcat holes.

The Ad Club didn't test out their first choice, because it would have meant hauling coal 18 miles for the drill rig. They decided to drill the second choice. There was one hitch. It had chosen a site owned by the Hudson's Bay Company at Brant. But instead of going to the trouble of trying to make a deal with the Bay for mineral rights, the Ad Club decided to drill in a field owned by Lars Salverson 4½ miles northwest of Viking.

Shades of the mix-up in drill sites at Bow Island No. 1.

When the Clapp and Huntley report was received, the Ad Club had organized the Edmonton Industrial Association Drilling Company Limited and sold shares.

In a repeat of Camrose, Martin and Phillips grabbed a contract away from a rival after it was promised. The deal was first promised to James Peat and Son Ltd. of Petrolia, Ont. But because Martin and Phillips came in with a better deal, a new contract was inked with them March 9, 1914, for Viking No. 1 and several other wells.

A reminder of bygone days in the Viking area.

There was some cash around to get the first well going but nobody knew how much; it was likely $25,000.

There was a small sod-turning ceremony the day the well was spudded in. Tiny Phillips remembers clearly what Magrath said:

"Exploitation for gas is only a secondary matter with the Ad Club. We intend to place a family on every quarter-section within 100 miles and make Edmonton the largest manufacturing city in the West."

This chamber of commerce-type boosterism, indeed pushed Edmonton toward becoming one of Canada's great cities and the surrounding area to becoming one of Canada's most prosperous agricultural communities. However, the farmer-on-every-quarter notion plagued later generations, as that pattern of settlement proved too small for viable farm operation, even on the good farmland. Quarter-section farmers weren't the kind who could adequately support a manufacturing industry. Their economy was based on the mail-order catalogue.

Edmonton never became the manufacuturing city Magrath envisioned either, because of the area's lack of basic raw materials suitable for rural population needs.

While all other business aspects of the Viking well deal were handled with acumen, the Ad Club overlooked one point that was

Once in camp the wives of drillers were forced to stick pretty close to "home".

to spell trouble later and delay the installation of gas for Edmonton for nearly a decade. There was an understanding between the Ad Club and the city council, that if gas were struck in commerical quantities the city was to take over the well. This understanding was never put into writing — and neither was the capriciousness of a voting public taken into consideration. Both factors caused a great deal of grief.

To say, however, the city did not have a direct interest is not true. James Brodie, the city's gas engineer, was on the site in a supervisory capacity. He lived in a tent with his wife and two children.

By the middle of summer, a small colony had sprung up near the wellsite. There were several cottages and six tents. In one of the "cottages" lived Garrett W. Green, the head driller, and his new bride. They had been married while the rig and tools were being moved from Camrose.

There was lots of time for such social activities. Johnston reported in his paper, the cars of machinery had been on the road two weeks from Medicine Hat and Camrose. He attributed the delay to "the slovenly manner in which the CPR handled the shipment and this has occasioned much adverse comment from many sources."

The Green's nuptial nest, was a one-room 14x16 tarpaper shack, made with some lumber bought at the Viking lumber yard. When Green was transferred to Wetaskiwin in July, they sold it to a bachelor farmer. He lived in it until his death in the early 1930s. The same linoleum the Greens had laid, was still on the floor.

In the tents were C.A. Flickinger and his wife; M. Skippen, the fireman, his wife and daughter; J. Joyce, tool dresser; J. McDonald, driller, and Red Columbus, fireman. J.S. Jamison, Frosty Martin's father-in-law, was the tool dresser and he divided his time between the Viking and Wetaskiwin wells. Also in camp was a Chinese cook, Mah Yee.

During her later life Mrs. Green admitted she suffered some privations in the rough, hard pioneering life, "but I wouldn't have missed a minute of it, with those swashbuckling crews which swept from one job to another.

"We would often have to move with two hours' notice. We moved 11 times in the first eight years. That's what made life endurable: the unexpected situation would crop up tomorrow. It was a roving life; here today; gone tomorrow.

"The Americans were expert liars about their qualifications when they showed up in Canada. Findlay roustabouts suddenly became firemen; firemen back there could get jobs as tool dressers and tool dressers could easily pass for drillers here."

After the outbreak of war, many returned to the new oil boom in Texas. The boom pushed wages to $20 for an eight-hour shift, (not 12 hours). But even though the drillers made 35 cents an hour in Alberta, they earned more in a month than neighboring farmhands or apprentices saw in a year.

The big pay days made up for the lonely existence of the women in the drilling camps. Once in camp the driller's wives were forced to stick pretty close to "home." It was usually too far to walk to town and, since cars were few and far between, hitching a ride with a teamster was about the only way. Groceries were brought once a week by a livery stable man from the nearest town. The teamster was always made welcome around camp, as he was a good storehouse of news and gossip.

The women made it a point to get to Edmonton or Calgary once a month, when the monthly pay envelope arrived. There, for a few hours, it was possible to visit the shops or friends and catch up on the news and everything else that had been missing, during the past month. Then back to the country on the local train.

There was usually a car for the "convenience of the camp," to get to the nearest post office or telephone. Naturally when the snow and zero weather came and the roads were blocked, the car was useless.

There was no thought of driving cars in winter. The men drained the water from the radiator in the fall to prevent radiators from cracking and left them to sit out during the cold months.

During rainy weather the roads were quagmires and the camp team was more reliable. Or, they relied on the livery from town.

About a quarter of a mile out of Viking, there was a drainage ditch to carry water away from the low-lying areas and sloughs. This ditch didn't have a bridge and usually Old Betty, the open-top Buick, was able to make it. But occasionally she didn't — and the rear end was left in the water. This meant going to get Steve Jones, the liveryman, and his mules to pull her out — both going and coming.

The car made as many miles behind his mules as it did under its own power that spring. Jone's six span of mules were a local institution for awhile and when one got tangled in a rope and strangled itself, it rated a small obit in the local paper. In her recollections, Mrs. Green said further:

"We had variety in this kind of life — from rattlesnakes in the Bow Island country, to the beautifully wooded foothill country; and we loved it all. Early Alberta was a wonderful place for children. There was so much for them to do outdoors.

"Admittedly the snakes often scared the life out of us in the south,

Typical prairie road in 1912.

Life was not all a bowl of oil on the Prairies. Woman unidentified. Photo circa 1919.

but the men who had seen them in the southern U.S. apparently had no fear of them and would pick them up.

"The most prevalent pest was the mosquitoes. They came out of every pothole. And the only known repellent we knew then was oil of citronella. It was bought by the gallon for the camp."

After travelling in various oilfields, Green moved back to Viking in 1925, as field superintendent, when the new Northwestern Utilities Company began piping gas to Edmonton. They lived there 13 years. The company built them a nice house at Viking, the only one in town with a bathroom and running water. That was just reward after years of living and roughing it in tarpaper shacks and tents. By then the oil patch was beginning to become an economic force in the new young province.

15

Oil Strike Near Olds

The Ad Club had some difficulty in keeping up its payments to the drillers, it was noted by Tiny Phillips in his well-worn scribbler. Money was harder to come by after the war started Aug. 5. The spectre of financial breakdown hung over the project until Oct. 24.

When the drillers got to within a few feet of where they thought they would strike gas, Tiny and Frosty went to Edmonton and called a meeting of the Ad Club to attempt to obtain some back pay. They made it clear they would simply have to shut down, if they didn't see any money. There were many glum faces when the club directors were told that since it was costing them $200 a day to run the drill rig, (a somewhat exaggerated figure), they would pull out. If the club could produce $1,000 cash, they would run the week out.

The combination of blarney and bluff worked. The directors scrounged around and came up with $1,000. The scribbler:

"Everyone went home feeling better, not to mention relieved we were going to keep on drilling. I went to a hotel for the night. At midnight Flickinger called me all excited. They had struck gas and had a three million cubic foot flow."

Fairly jumping with excitement, Tiny got dressed and called up Magrath. He came over to hear the good news.

"He called up all the boys. They all came to the hotel immediately. There was little sleep that night. J.F. Phillip, the Grand Trunk Pacific superintendent, was called out of bed to arrange a special train for Viking to visit the well Sunday."

Included on the passenger list was one Mr. Robinson who was simply listed as a "capitalist."

H.G. Thunnell, the new editor of The Times, came out with a double-deck streamer headline to announce the find. Intoxicating as the news was, Martin and Phillips decided it could be better by drilling the discovery well deeper. They took a calculated risk, in the form of 1,000 shares of stock in the Edmonton Association Drilling Company, that deeper drilling would pay off. It did — prompting Thunnell to get out the type reserved for the Second Coming of Christ, to

Sod turning ceremony for Viking No. 1 well, March 11, 1914. A.P. Phillips, second from left W.J. McGrath, President of Edmonton Industrial Association, with spade. Photo: Glenbow Archives, Calgary, Alberta.

On the site of the No. 2 Viking well. Individuals in group photo include in back row, left to right, Steve Adams, Driller; Frosty Martin, Karl Klentsche, Driller; Andy Ruthford, Tool Dresser. Front Row (L to R) Steve Jones, Freighter; Photographer; Cook (unidentified); youngster on unidentified man's knee is Buzz Jones, Peanut Adams far right.

announce a flow of nine million feet had been brought in Nov. 4, 1914.

On that night, Flickinger again raced to the Viking telegraph office on his motor bike with the news. Frosty and Jamison came down on the noon train next day and Frosty pronounced Edmonton a "favoured city." But back in Edmonton, some skepticism developed over his claim, because he had been involved in two wells in the Calgary area which had been salted. There was also opposition to gas from the coal lobby, which kept up a drumfire of wild untrue rumours and anit-gas agitiation. The coal dealers shouted against the city ratifying the unwritten agreement, with the Ad Club to take over the well.

To allay the skepticism, the Ad Club chartered another special train from the GTP and hauled 173 businessmen to Viking, Nov. 7. When the train arrived at 4.30 p.m., it was a clear, cold autumn day. The expectant crowd was greeted on the station program by the local concert band.

The Viking Board of Trade had persuaded nearby farmers to leave their cattle and supply rigs, democrats and wagons to transport the trainload to the well. Along with a number of cars loaned by Vikingites

Workers at Viking No. 2 well, Viking. Extreme left, Karl Klentsche; extreme right, squatting, W.R. Martin.

themselves, the imposing procession stretched half a mile. In one of the lead cars, was Lieut.-Gov. George Bulyea of Alberta. He and other personalities provided camera fodder for the large contingent of still and movie cameramen on hand.

Frosty Martin was there in all his glory. It gave him the greatest satisfaction of his life to turn on gas. Reports written by Tiny in the scribbler said, "the gas burst forth with a roar from the bowels of the earth, where it had been imprisoned for eons. The noise was terrific and the crowd scattered as if some terrible monster had been let loose. Some held their ears. The demonstration clearly dispelled any doubts that gas abounded and that the strike was not a genuine one. A more pleased man than Frosty was not to be found on the grounds."

Frosty, however, had one more choice bit of showmanship up his sleeve. It proved the biggest event of the evening. Just after the sun set and the cold took hold of the soul-stirred group, he turned gas into a pipe laid 100 feet from the well. He lit the gushing gas with a torch. The flames shot high into the air to the cheers of the crowd. The flames spread light and warmth over the group.

At the December elections, the ratepayers repudiated council action on provision of $150,000 for No. 1 and drilling more to get an estimate of the size of the field.

Martin and Phillips had no other recourse than to file two mechanics liens totalling $38,000, against the land on which the wells were drilled.

Then they sent a hurry-up call to Eugene Coste at Calgary to take over the well and persuade council to issue a gas distribution

Frosty and Tiny make newspaper headlines with their Viking well progress.

franchise. Council decided to go to the ratepayers again with a reduced money bylaw for $36,000. Another special train carrying 100, was despatched to Viking to prove there actually was a well there. But in March, 1915, they turned it down a second time.

Knowing that he was not likely to see reorganization of the faltering Edmonton Industrial Association Drilling Company and, because of the way things were going, Edmonton Council was never going to take over the area and develop the plant, Frosty Martin searched about for some private capital interested in exploiting the Viking field. With the assistance of W.H. McLaws, the Calgary lawyer, Leigh Hunt, a Kansas City capitalist, and T.A. McAuley, a Calgary wholesaler, he set up the Northern Alberta Natural Gas Development Company Limited (NANGDC), March 31, 1915, with the four as directors.

This move brought a couple of competitive elements out of the woodwork. They were the Pelican Oil and Gas Company of which H.L. Williams of Edmonton was manager, and Northwest Drilling Company. As a matter of fact, both these companies had been invited by the Edmonton Council to make similar deals with it, as the Edmonton Industrial Association Drilling Company did in 1914, after the city fathers saw the rival, Calgary, had been successful in piping gas from Bow Island.

Northwest Drilling had brought in a small well at Vegreville, before Martin and Phillips had managed to bring in Viking No. 1.

Pelican and its predecessors, on the other hand, had begun operations in 1896, when the Geological Survey of Canada had undertaken a drilling program in Alberta, to prove the existence of oil and gas. It brought in a shallow well at Athabasca (334 feet), 100 miles north of Edmonton that year. The next year it drilled at Pelican Rapids, at the confluence of the Athabaska and Pelican Rivers, 90 miles downstream from Athabasca. They ran into a tremendous flow of gas and tar sands in that well. The well caught fire and burned 21 years — a landmark in the area. Other successful wells were drilled, with production large enough to satisfy Edmonton's needs.

And so when Edmonton signified it was ready to sign a city franchise, Pelican made a formal application for the franchise March, 31, 1915, the same day as NANGDC was incorporated. Pelican was given the franchise in October. They got the nod, despite the fact Clapp and Huntley predicted the life of the Pelican field would be shorter than the other two and its gas costs higher.

However, when Pelican observed the flow of gas from the nearby well at Viking and the fact the Ad Club was having financial problems, it effected a merger with Frosty Martin's NANGDC, mostly for the purpose of developing the Viking field to supply the Edmonton franchise.

In the meantime, Alberta Volcanic Oil Company Ltd. was brought into the picture. This company was the creation of Eugene Coste.

As the man who had successfully brought gas to Calgary, Martin asked him to take a hand in bringing it to Edmonton. The part Alberta Volcanic played at this time, was to go quietly into the field and acquire gas leases and rights over a wide area during the summer of 1915.

Back in Edmonton, things were not going smoothly. The coal dealer lobby succeeded in having the vote delayed, on a bylaw to grant the gas franchise to Pelican or Northern Natural Gas Development. The coal men brought in F.T. Dixon MPP, of Winnipeg, to speak against the agreement. But the gas company brought in its big guns, too, in the person of McLaws. However, in a vote taken Nov. 11, 1915, all opposition was beaten back and the bylaw was carried, on the basis that the company had the option of supplying gas from Viking or at Pelican Rapids. For its part in the deal, Pelican was allotted $400,000 worth of stock in NANGDC. The franchise agreement stipulated the company was to supply gas for 25 cents per 1,000 for domestic and 15 cents for industrial purposes.

Prior to the vote NANGDC increased its capitalization to $6 million, made up by the addition of 55,000 shares at $100 each. McLaws loaned the company $32,000 to continue drilling, to prove up the field at the same time. At the end of November, H.L. Williams, now NANGDC manager, announced in Viking he had given orders to Bert Ruble to get going on another derrick for No. 2 well. With shareholders beginning to invest money in the new company, it had been possible to pay off the mechanic's lien held by International Supply Company. Martin continued as a director until 1917. By that time Eugene Coste and son, Dillon, had taken over management and moved the head office to Calgary to be near their other company, Canadian Western Natural Gas. In 1916-17, Martin and Phillips continued drilling wells to define the boundaries of the Viking field.

By the time the company was ready to construct its Viking-Edmonton pipeline, costs had risen to the point where it was impossible to supply the city with gas, at rates agreed upon in the original franchise. The great demand for steel, scarcity of labour and the impossibility of obtaining construction equipment, (engendered by the war), had sent costs in an inflationary spiral.

The city and company were in a stalemate over the issue for five years. Of course, the coal lobby was jubilant and encouraged continuation of the stalemate.

Finally the city asked the old Board of Public Utility Commissioners of Alberta to step in to act as arbitrators. The board ruled, in late 1922, the city should pay for gas based on a domestic rate of 46½ cents.

However, it took one more reorganization of the company to acquire the necessary $4 million. NANGDC had started to "come apart at the seams" when the Coste family, for an unexplained reason, picked up and returned to Toronto. With the company operating rudderless, the shareholders met in 1923 and sold control to Northwestern Utilities Limited, a companion company of Canadian Western Natural Gas. The head office was moved to Edmonton and work on the line began in 1923.

The 77-mile transmission line and 80 miles of distributor lines were completed in just 116 working days. By the end of the year 1,900 customers were hooked up.

The arrival of gas was marked with a big ceremony, in which Mayor D.M. Duggan opened a valve and lighted a huge flare. As far as Edmonton has been concerned: from that date onward the flare has never gone out.

By that time Frosty and Tiny were long gone, the former from Canada forever.

Chapter 16

George E. Buck's Heavenly Kingdom

The people around Edmonton knew Tiny and Frosty had been involved in the drilling of two oil wells in the Calgary area which had been salted, i.e., oil was brought up in the bailer, which had been sent down in the bailer, by somebody.

The hysteria which accompanied the Turner Valley oil boom, was responsible for the unseemly conduct of promotors trying to maintain or boost share prices, following the flurry of excitement occasioned by high-grade oil in the Dingman discovery well at Turner Valley Oct. 9, 1913.

The Calgarians engaged in the salting at the two spurious wells were William Georgeson, a tea, coffee and spice wholesaler, and George E. Buck, a revival preacher.

When the Dingman well showed indications of tapping into an oil pool, Georgeson formed a syndicate which hired B.W. Dunn, a graduate of the Houghton, Mich., School of Mines, to lease the mineral rights on 56,000 acres in the area west of Olds near Sundre.

The Georgeson syndicate did things in a big way, as the 25-cent-an-acre lease amounting to $14,000 was the largest sum ever received in one day at the Calgary land office.

The syndicate had also applied for gas franchises in Moose Jaw and Regina to be served with gas piped from Bow Island. But Eugene Coste put a damper on that idea in 1912; he said it was too far. It was then but not later.

In the centre of the lease, Dunn selected a site for the well he named the Monarch. He was so confident oil was there he put $4,800 of his own money into the syndicate.

Tiny and Frosty were hired to drill the well and 11 others.

By May 24, 1914, they were down to 700 feet.

Oil excitement had reached fever pitch in Calgary and was beginning to taper off somewhat. This flurry was caused May 6, when

Archibald Wayne Dingman the Toronto soap maker and pioneer in the Alberta oil industry at Turner Valley. Photo: Glenbow Archives, Calgary, Alberta.

Buck had salted his Black Diamond No. 1 well. On May 14, the Dingman well came in with large production and the city went wild. But by the middle of June the excitement had died down; in fact, the boom almost died on its feet — and a shot in the arm was needed.

The shot was provided June 17 when Dunn called a group of directors to the wellsite and announced that black oil was struck at a depth of 808 feet. An official announcement to that effect was published in The Morning Albertan June 18.

The "newsbreak" was given to the loquacious managing editor, William W. Cheely — a type of reporter for which The Albertan and its successor, The Calgary Sun, have always had a reputation. Cheely became part of this story and others, in which he assisted promotors fly kites and kept the whole city in ferment and frenzy for some months. He came in from Great Falls, Montana. His story of June 18 said in part:

"Geologist Dunn immediately ordered a cessation of drilling operations, fearing that if the bit should cut further into oil-bearing stratum a gusher would result.

"Drilling wil not be resumed until a special appliance, which will permit the drilling to be continued with the well capped, has been sent from Medicine Hat. Tiny Phillips, the head driller, a man of many years experience, said a shot of nitroglycerine would bring a gusher of sufficient strength to blow down the derrick."

Georgeson and Dunn filled Cheely in on the events leading up to the bailer coming up with oil in it. He wrote column after column of fulsome copy, plus sidebars and talked of "the wonder that had happened."

The strike was well timed. It came the day following the date set by the directors for a stock dividend. All holders of the original stock were entitled to as many shares of record on June 15, at par, stock being issued share for share. The second block of 100,000 shares was put on the market. This stock went to old subscribers, on deferred payments, the first being due July 15.

Cheely revealed Monarch stock had jumped to $40 from $8--" and the certainty exists here in Alberta is one of the great oil fields of the world."

He was right, except that he was 35 years ahead of his time and 45 years in that particular district. Nor did he count upon two world wars entering into his prognostication.

The same morning — June 18 — The Albertan had a grab bag of other stories on the front page about the accelerated boom created by the Monarch well. They were designed to send the small investor racing hysterically for his bank account.

"Largest field in the world," says O.S. Chapin. Chapin owned a large car dealership, a big feed company and was a director in Calgary Petroleum Products, the company which drilled the Dingman well.

Equal weight was given another story about Miss F.M. Hudson, a clerk in the natural resources department of the CPR, who had received $54,000 and a great block of stock for a 480-acre lease. The Albertan reporter found her at her desk that day, notwithstanding her newfound wealth and revealed she planned to keep on working. The story added:

"You know, there are many well-to-do employees of the CPR. I have worked so long I wouldn't know what to do with myself if I quit work. Perhaps after I have had time to build a house and buy a car, I will be able to enjoy luxurious idleness.

"It is not necessary for me to tell you how I happened to pick out a lease right on the anticline. I know all about anticlines and it was not all chance. I do not know who bought the mineral rights, as I acted through an agent, but I understand it was a Montreal syndicate. I have the money in the bank and the syndicate is going to drill two wells right away. That was a provision I insisted upon."

The knowledgeable Miss Hudson — it was remarkable how even women clerks were becoming geological experts — retained 160 acres and hoped to get as much for it as the lease she sold.

Invited to visit the well, Cheely went to Olds by train, then was taken to the Monarch camp by chauffeured limousine. His return journey was filled with bitter hardships. When he phoned in from Olds, an Albertan rewrite man thought it worth a story in itself. Being able to spot a cockalorum, he wrote a story headed: "Bill Cheely's Awful Journey."

"Say, son, stop the press. We had an awful time getting back to the well from Olds."

It was Bill Cheely's voice on the phone at midnight and it sounded hoarse and sepulchral — in keeping with the witching hour.

Bill let it be known rain had fallen heavily in the vicinity of the Monarch well and he insinuated the roads were so sticky with mud it had been necessary for him to carry the car a mile or so at a time. Otherwise his chauffeur might have perished.

However, he admitted he had managed to secure the bridal suite in the best hotel in Olds and was endeavoring, to the best of his ability, to forget the bitter hardships of the journey on behalf of this newspaper that for pure, unadulterated bravery and heroism far surpassed that made by Capt. Cook in the frozen islands of the gumdrop country.

Incidentally, Bill was so worked up about the prospects of the oilfield, that the telephone operator became alarmed and cut the connection, just as he was in the act of stating that the oilfield smelled to him more sweetly, than all the perfumes that could have ever emanated from the gardens of Araby.

Cheely quoted Dunn as saying the Monarch strike would now mean oilmen all over the world will have "sufficient confidence in the future of the petroleum industry in Alberta, to put their millions into it for the necessary development."

Yes, the oil stock prices took a jump but not as much as they had during the Dingman coming in during May. One citizen who had been out of work for some time and around whose door the wolves of starvation had hovered, sold 150 shares of Monarch stock for $6,750 — or $45 a share. He had paid $1 each "when times were good."

But this couldn't happen in Olds: "Shareholders there won't sell their stock at any price."

Three other salutary effects outlined by Cheely:

"Olds didn't go to bed last night."

"The Olds Gazette, which never runs anything but ads on the front page, swept some off this week and broke out with a blackface box: STRIKE."

"Even in the church synod sessions in Calgary today, gentlemen in cassocks were seen surreptitiously reading the latest bulletins."

Alas, the showing of oil proved so small it was decided to drill deeper. Martin and Phillips took it to 3,800 feet. When Georgeson ran out of money and couldn't pay them $5,000 he owed, drilling was stopped.

The company went broke in 1916.

George E. Buck was the other Calgarian who salted a well which Tiny and Frosty drilled. He was a glib-talking revival preacher who began coining money by the pailful in the Calgary bucket shops in the frantic oil boom of 1914. The Calgary oil patch has never really lived down the black name those pre-war stockateers gave it. Buck's motive for relieving the "suckers" of their money, was the same one that has always motivated preachers who seek the Holy Grail, to establish a kingdom of heaven on earth in the foothills of the Rockies.

As happens with many persons of advanced age, Tiny compressed a drama, whose central character was Buck, into his scribbler in a few paragraphs. It was a tableau much more historic and occupying much longer in time than the old driller noted down:

"Martin and Phillips took a contract to drill a well for the Black Diamond Oil Company, the first contract and well up Sheep Creek.

"George E. Buck was president of the company and promotor, (some promoter!). He took the well over at 1,800 feet, formed his own company, the Jennie Earl Drilling Company, bought some tools, hired one of the drillers we had brought in from Findlay and started up. In a couple of weeks of pumping up and down in the hole they hit pay sand — but not in the hole or well. Buck shipped oil in by the can, salted the hole and made a fortune and wound up in jail. This was the first production sold by the bottle, to encourage suckers to buy stock.

"Buck sold stock to keep us drilling. He had to pay us every 100 feet but could not keep up the payments — so when we reached 1,800 feet we shut down to get our money. He made a new deal, promising to pay us each week from the proceeds of stock sales. But he owed us $12,000.

"One Saturday night, I came into Calgary and told Buck we were going to move the rig. Later he and his partner came to Medicine Hat to make arrangements to leave the outfit there for another week. We did.

"I was drilling around Viking at the time. I came back to Calgary the following Friday night and stayed over at a hotel. Saturday morning, when I went downstairs, the girl at the switchboard told me they had struck oil at the Black Diamond well.

"I asked her who told her and she said Buck had brought oil to town which had been pumped out of the well. While we were standing there one of my friends, a newspaper reporter, came in and asked me if I had any of the Black Diamond stock for sale.

"As a matter of fact, I had 200 shares Buck had given me. This was one of the few times I ever owned stock in a well I was drilling. I never made it a practice to invest in a wildcat hole.

"Then he told me Buck was giving vials of oil away. He claimed Buck had drilled the hole deeper. I tried to tell the fellows he was lying, because we had taken away the tools and he couldn't drill a foot deeper. We had taken the crew off the job, all except one driller we left as watchman.

"I went to Buck's office to see him. When I got there it was crowded with people buying stock. He met me and took me into his back office and paid me the $12,000 he owed me. He said he had drilled a few feet further and got oil. We had quite an argument as to his drilling.

"Anyway, I went down to the well and found the driller. He said Buck had brought the oil out and had him run the bailer and that Buck had put the oil in the barrel when he dumped the bailer. He had brought some people down from Calgary and showed them the oil. He had skimmed the oil off the top of the water and put it in vials and gave it to the people and told them he got the oil out of the well.

"Well, I took the driller to Calgary and he took the first train out of town for the States and I never heard of him again.

"I told my friends Buck did not do any more drilling and did not get any oil out of that particular hole. However, my words did not seem to have any effect on the investing public. They were buying up stock like mad."

Chapter 17

The Salted Oil Well at Turner Valley

George *Edward Buck* was born March 20, 1867, one of nine children of an Ontario farmer. His birthplace was Esquesing Township in the County of Halton. From an early age, he was brought up on a farm at the corner of the Third Line and No. 5 Side Road in Trafalgar Township, now part of the City of Oakville. His early background belied many of his latter activities — except in the particular that he was a devoutly religious man who knew his Bible from cover to cover.

The farm boy in the 1870s in Ontario had anything but an easy life. He was usually part of a large family, because the cashless economy of that day, dictated that large families were a necessity for provision of a cheap labour pool. The custom of the day decreed that each son labour on the farm until he reached his majority. What schooling he received was on a catch-as-catch-can basis at a one-room rural school. The chief source of reading material was the Bible. Work was from dawn to dusk, six days a week and little Sunday activity, except church-going, was possible because of strict blue laws.

And so it was against this background of hard work, little education and rigid conformity, that we find George Buck leaving the farm in his early 20s to seek out a new life in the commercial world. He had the brains and the personality to establish himself well in the insurance field in Toronto. He found the big city a less-inhibiting place than the farm. There were more opportunities to make an honest dollar — at least in selling insurance. He married Ada Beattie of a well-known Toronto family; niece of James Beattie, a one-time Toronto mayor. They had a family of five.

But George Buck had a dream — the vision of uniting sect-ridden Protestantism into the Church of Christ — to restore the primitive church known by Jesus Christ's followers. This dream transcended the comfortable but rigid, circumstances in which he found himself in Toronto. He knew he could never make this dream come true in Toronto the Good, (but hypocritical).

He had become imbued with the zeal of Thomas Campbell of Pennsylvania, to go to the Western frontier to realize the dream. Campbell was a pioneer of the Church of Christ. The Buck family were acquainted with him as they had originated in Bucks County, Pennsylvania. They came to Canada as United Empire Loyalists. At least one branch of the family did not maintain the British tradition; Tim Buck branched off to become leader of the Communist Party of Canada.

The peccant* wide open cow town of Calgary was a ready-made haven, for the talents of Buck, when he stepped off the CPR transcontinental train one fine day in 1907. He was sent to Calgary by the Manufacturers Life Insurance Company as superintendent of its branch there: very shortly he switched to New York Life. He was the kind of man who could make his way in a frontier city, a stout man of medium height, good-looking, an impressive talker who exuded confidence all over the place, ambitious and enterprising, a complete extrovert.

It was not long after Buck arrived in Calgary that he began to lead a small group of followers in the tradition of the Church of Christ, (Disciples). The small flock held meetings in the old army drill hall and after a while in a tent by the river. Later a small church was built at the corner of 15th Ave. and 6th St. S.W., (it was razed in 1962 to make room for an apartment block).

The Disciples combined a maximum of spiritual freedom with a minimum of churchly trappings. Buck soon found himself freed of other bounds that had contained him in the East. He made an impressive appearance around town dressed in a black broadcloth coat and soft dark hat. A small waxed mustache adorned his upper lip. Business was good and he took time to go fishing on some of the virgin creeks around Black Diamond and Turner Valley. There he saw geological strata and oil slicks on the waters, much like he had seen on a visit to oil-rich Oklahoma.

Standing alone in the wilderness silences, he saw the grand dream of a great Christian empire arise, with oil as its financial lifeblood and he as head of the church. It was not the first time the grand expansive foothills country has had that effect on a man and it won't be the last.

---

* sinful

The chance to make money to make the dream come true, came in Calgary's real estate boom in 1910. Buck organized a real estate company B and R Co. Ltd., in 1910, with an office in the new Patrick Burns Building.

An impressively printed letterhead indicated the city had grown to 55,000 from 19,000 in three years.

Success in business gave Buck an addiction to big flashy cars. His red Dodge was one of the few autos on Calgary's narrow cow-trail streets. He used tobacco in pipes and cigars. The tobacco habit seemed strangely out of place for a minister of the gospel, especially in his austere church. He gave generously of his time to the small church and probably more money than he could afford, as sometimes his family went short. He would bring home anyone with a hard-luck story for a meal or a bed. Some often stayed on for several weeks — to the consternation of the family. He was a wonderful minister and highly thought of by his followers.

Through the real estate company he had acquired an interest in a coal mining property on Wolf Creek, near Black Diamond. Black Diamond was then a general store five miles east of Turner Valley, at the junction of the road heading up Sheep Creek. Development of the mine revealed it contained only a coal pocket rather than a seam as anticipated.

When the oil and gas staking rush occurred in October, 1913, following the first showings in the Dingman well, Buck was in on the ground floor. In the name of his real estate firm, he acquired several oil leases along the Sheep River and organized a syndicate to exploit them. The syndicate, called the Coalinga Oil Syndicate, consisted of Buck, wife Ada, John A. Campbell, and Jennie L. Earl.

The origin of "Coalinga" probably stemmed from the Coalinga foothills in the St. Joaquin Valley, 120 miles north-west of Los Angeles, where a six-billion-barrel oilfield was discovered by the famour wildcatter, Charles Canfield, in 1895. It was only coincidental, too, that Coalinga Syndicate was the name of a California company with whom C. Naramore was associated previously and who was then "operating manager," Calgary Petroleum Products.

Wells in the Coalinga field, plus other rich fields in California and Texas brought total U.S. production up to 86 million barrels annually by 1912. This amount exeeded production of all other oil countries. Fantastic valuations were placed on oil-producing properties by 1912. In that year, California Oil Fields Ltd. paid $565,000 for 480 acres in the Coalinga field. It later sold this interest to Shell Oil for $12½ million.

Tagged with a famous name like Coalinga, Buck had great expectations for the inauguration of his pioneer oil production venture.

The Coalinga Oil Syndicate proceeded to peddle its lease to a public corporation, Black Diamond Oil Fields Ltd., which Buck organized and was president. Black Diamond took in money and paid it out to Coalinga for leases it owned. Many other companies resorted to this suspect method of financing. This drew condemnation in the financial community, that investors were being subjected to unnecessary risks by oil companies drilling in unproven fields. Heading the critics was Col. J.H. Woods, editor of The Calgary Herald.

Woods' condemnation of Buck slowed down the flow of dollars into Black Diamond coffers. However, by borrowing from his friends, relatives and employees, including his wife, Jennie Earl, his sister-in-law and others, Buck had enough money by Nov. 29, 1913, to persuade Tiny and Frosty to drill three wells on the lease. The drill started Jan. 29, 1914.

Drilling proceeded well during the winter, but for reasons best known to himself, Buck couldn't put his hands on enough money to keep up with drilling installments. He became so desperate for new funds, he began using his employees to panhandle their relatives. Norman Fletcher, general office factotum, was a native of St Marys, Ont. He came to Alberta in 1912 and went to work for Buck in March, 1914. From time to time he was susceptible to illness and took to his bed in the Colonial Rooms. However, he wasn't too sick to write to an uncle, Edward Flach, of Shakespeare, Ont., at Buck's behest and persuade him to buy 4,000 shares in stock on a promise of $1,000 bonus.

However, such devotion as Fletcher's wasn't enough. Buck had been warned by his lawyers, Bennett, Lougheed and McLaws, that if the money was not ready, proceedings could be taken by Martin and Phillips to close down the operation. Little stock was being sold in Black Diamond and shareholders were beginning to ask some embarrassing questions.

Buck acted to overcome this situation May 7, when he invited Ald. E.H. Crandell, a trustee appointed by the shareholders, to lead a party to inspect the site. He had come to the realization no more money could be raised until an oil discovery caused a boom. In desperation, he decided to put some crude oil, gasoline and distillate into the well for the benefit of Ald. Crandell. Most of the office staff were in on this plan, including Harry C. Beatty, company advertising manager, and Elizabeth Beattie, Buck's mother-in-law. She had a lot of money sunk in the venture. Another was Roy Gourlay, a stock salesman, who obtained the materials. Major William Gillespie of Vulcan, Alta., of the 21st Alberta Hussars, was another salesman involved. The actual salting was done by Ray Minue, fireman at the well, and a tool dresser, L.L. Terrill.

On the appointed day Ald. Crandell, accompanied by Ald. Stanley

G. Freeze, Charles Tryon, manager of the News-Telegram and W.W. Cheely of the Morning Albertan, were shown a barrel of oil or a liquid that looked like oil. The drillers said they had got it out of the well the night before. Buck burned some of the stuff in a pail and also lit a match over the end of the drill pipe and it flamed up. Tryon questioned Hayes closely about the "discovery," but couldn't get any satisfactory information from him.

Buck approached Tryon to phone his editor, Charles Hayden, from Black Diamond and ask him to put out a special edition announcing the "strike." Tryon said it would cost $50 to $450 to get out a special edition. Buck agreed to pay the cost and also offered to give him some stock in Black Diamond. Tryon refused to go along with such a plan, although the paper did print a small story on the "strike" May 8.

Buck had expected big black headlines and when he didn't get them he called Tryon and sarcastically berated him. He henceforth gave all his stories and ads to Cheely, whose paper used American-style sensationalism.

The "quick buck boys" like George E. got a big break May 18, when Dingman No. 1 came in at 2,178 feet, with 200 barrels a day of high-grade oil. It was so near the gasoline fraction it would run cars.

The papers brought the moribund boom back with big stories in studhorse Gothic type. A new wave of stock buying made the real estate boom look like a mere trifle. Being a new type of enterprise in Alberta, the average person didn't know much about its nature except that it could make him rich.

Chapter 18

A.F.A. Coyne's
Fellowship With Farmer

*P*romotors started stories to the effect there was enough oil in southern Alberta to satisfy the whole world; the south country was fairly teeming with it; it was sprouting out of the ground.

At the height of the boom the following year (1915) oldtimers who had been in the Yukon Gold Rush, said Dawson City was a quiet town compared to Calgary. Every man, woman and child wanted to invest in oil; it was actually the surplus earnings of the common man that provided the risk capital; debts to grocers and other merchants went unpaid, as people sought out the 500 oil companies which came into existence and literally thrust money upon them. Oil companies and brokerage offices sprang up overnight — and not a few disappeared just as quickly. This was easily done as all there was to leave behind, was their name on a sign outside the door, a desk, several wastepaper baskets, a book of stock certificates and the unpaid rent. This is not to say there were no honest companies. There were. Many still exist in some form or other today.

The hardest working people in town were the printers. They worked night and day turning out fancy gilt-edged gold-sealed stock certificates. The sign painters worked overtime too, to design window signs with different new catch phrases and slogans. Every vacant store and office suite was snapped up at fancy prices. Every office building housed two or three oil companies. When pants pockets and cash drawers became full of folding money, there was no place else to store the green flow but in wastepaper baskets. Stock certificates were issued as fast as clerks could enter the names of investors.

Brokers' offices were open six days a week night and day. The seventh day they were closed in observance of the blue laws. Police Chief Alf Cuddy, pharisee that he was, made it known that he would prosecute anyone given to the temptation of making oil stock transactions on the Lord's Day. His policeman's mentality could countenance the perpetration of fraud on a wide scale, only so long as it wasn't done on Sunday. He couldn't countenance the public outrage of breaking Sunday observance which, after all, was one form of law which he could enforce for the grandstand packed with zealots and from which there was no appeal.

Cuddy stalked the downtown district of a Sunday in plain clothes, "camping on the trail of several prospective buyers who appeared on the warpath."

While everyone else seemed to get all the attention and dollars needed, in the 12 days after the Crandell trip to the well, all was doom and gloom in the office of Black Diamond because Tiny Phillips and Frosty were threatening to shut down the drilling operation, if they didn't receive some money on account. Things were looking black for Black Diamond, so black that at one point Buck pulled his shares off the market. To get the money flowing again, he took on a couple of super-stock salesmen, in addition to the hangers-on around the office. One was Allan Clarke, farmer turned stock broker overnight with no previous experience in that game. The other was Fred C. Smith, a former advertising manager with The Albertan.

The two offered to organize an all-out promotion for a commission of 50 per cent. While that commission might seem exorbitant, it was standard for those days. Not only were big commissions offered, but bonus shares were given with every allotment as an inducement to attract purchasers.

The deal to sell the shares was made on the afternoon the Dingman well came in. Clarke and Buck had threshed out the details of the selling agreement, but nothing was ever put down in writing. Just as Buck's secretary, Jennie L. Earl, was ready to type out the agreement, Smith came in with the news of the strike. Buck dropped everything and went out to see what was happening and never came back.

This laxity set the pattern of business transactions from then on. The pair had to find a way of getting the stock onto the market, without letting people know it came directly from the office, since Buck had pulled it off the market. They took newspaper space to advertise that they had acquired a large block of shares, of a California capitalist, and were offering it for sale. The actual capitalist was Mrs. Elizabeth Beattie. Eleven thousand shares of Coalinga had been transferred to her in trust and these were the ones being sold.

Advertising manager Harry C. Beatty, wrote ads which were only partly true. However, everyone else was doing the same thing. So what?

Space was at a premium. The Albertan's newshole was 5% — about the same as 1989. It was able to ration space to a maximum of 24 pages and charged cash on the barrelhead for ads.

Money was thrown about with abandon. Customers forced their way up the stairs or accosted Clarke and Smith on the street, to lay money on them — money which they stuffed in their pockets and tried to keep accounts straight without books. They kept some and gave some to Jennie Earl. She gave them receipts but they never recorded them on paper. People were sending in $5 and $10 in envelopes. Some was not acknowledged.

These dissolute transactions were bound to lead to trouble. Clarke decided to make a selling trip to California, with $15,000 from the sales promotion account. In retaliation, Buck withheld his commissions. Clarke and Smith sued Buck for $30,000. Their case was dismissed many months later, on the grounds that they had kept no books to prove their claim.

Calgarians became a bit insane and ludicrous in their actions in the 1914 oil boom. No further proof was needed than the following exchange, which took place in the examination for discovery, of Buck in the Clarke and Smith lawsuit. Testimony brought out the fact, that one day Clarke was waiting for Buck, as he drew up to the Black Diamond office in his big red car. He wanted to press for payment of the commission.

Buck invited him into the car and they drove around the block to discuss the matter. They came back and stopped again at the oil office and went inside.

Buck was asked during the examination if he had any further conversation about the deal with Clarke, Buck answered yes.

Q. Did Clarke say he was going to fix it up with Smith?
A. He did not. The conversation came to an abrupt end.
Q. Why?
A. My Pipe exploded. Somebody loaded it and it exploded about that time.
Q. So you did not discuss commissions any further?
A. No, we did not discuss commissions any further.

With thousands of dollars at stake this was the irreverent and evasive way in which business was carried on.

Chapter 19

The Conspiracy Against Coyne

A *large number* of shareholder lawsuits were filed against Buck, for raiding the Black Diamond treasury and transferring the money fraudulently into Coalinga for his own use.

The question may be asked: why didn't the shareholders get together and oust him in a proxy battle, rather than going through the courts for injunctions? The answer is: Buck hadn't maintained a shareholder record in a manner that made it available to all.

Although at one point an injunction was issued against Buck restraining him from "dealing" in monies belonging to the Black Diamond company, provision was made to allow use of company funds to continue the drilling program.

While court action was pending, Buck hit back at the dissident shareholders and other critics by several means.

He organized an oil newspaper called the Black Diamond Press. For official purposes the paper was published by the Coalinga Syndicate.

He brought in a Saskatoon man, Vernon Knowles, as editor, and Basil J. Casey as business manager. Naturally, the paper carried news and advertising favorable to Black Diamond.

Despite this, the three daily newspapers were feeding the fires of oil-patch speculation with statements from Tiny Phillips, that International Supply Company had ordered 14 more strings of tools and Frosty Martin had gone to Pittsburgh, Pa., to expedite shipment of them. Tiny predicted, within a month the region surroundiong Calgary "will be a forest of derricks."

International Supply Company was about to set up a machine shop for well drillers in Okotoks.

On May 25, Buck ran a ad in The Calgary Herald to scourge the "liars" and "detractors," because Black Diamond No. 2 was going to come in and be a GIANT GUSHER. But although Tiny and Frosty had a contract to drill No. 2, they had not started and, in fact, did not do so until August.

The way he proceeded in his promotional campaign, Buck was 20 years ahead of Josef Goebbels using the "big lie."

In preparation for another salting venture June 23 — the one at which Tiny had caught him red-handed — Buck had hired W.W. Grant, a pioneer radio broadcaster and technician, to install a wireless telegraph sending set at the well and a receiving set at Calgary. The installation was active for about five months and was ready to send out the first word of the impending strike.

A section of Tiny's scribbler recounts how Buck sent visitors to the well in a big car schauffeured by Harold Hodgins:

"They found the works heavily guarded in much the same manner as a baronial castle. However, instead of pikes, the head guard, William Ernest Budge, carried an army service rifle.

"The well was surrounded by a ditch full of water and the river, and only after Buck gave a pass word was the drawbridge let down and the car was given safe conduct across the moat. The derricks in those days were built of wood and enclosed, so it was impossible to see what was going on inside.

"Budge was not averse to firing the rifle whenever unidentified people showed up., He would fire four or five rounds when visitors approached from the opposite bank of the Sheep River. This gave an air of mystery to the whole outfit. Buck encouraged this activity.

When an official party came on an inspection trip on his invitation, he ordered Budge to fire shots over their heads to give a good impression.

The second salting coincided with the Monarch well incident. From that time on things began to get rough for Buck. He therefore made a desperate grandstand play, to bring in outside money from Vancouver.

It came about when the governor-general, the Duke of Connaught, his wife and daughter Princes Patricia paid another state visit to the West, July 28 and stopped off at Calgary. They wre given a miniature golden oil derrick by the oil patch and taken on a trip to Turner Valley to inspect Dingman's discovery well, which was later sold to Imperial Oil Ltd.

Shortly after they left Calgary in a cavalcade of cars, the vice-regal party was corraled by another sight-seeing party led by none other than that mastermiond of spectacular and audacious publicity, George E. Buck. Photographers were strategically placed to record.

The party went to the Dingman well, where Ald. Tappy Frost gave a demonstration of drinking a cup of oil which, said the Natural Gas and Oil Record, he drinks every afternoon for medicinal purposes. A picture taken of the event is still reproduced around the world.

This was as much of the story as any of the Calgary papers used. Buck, in a frenzy because his "plot" to spirit the vice-regal party to his Black Diamond wells had failed, wired his version to the Vancouver World. The Natural Gas and Oil Record reprinted The World story in its Aug. 1, 1914, edition but labelled it "LIES! LIES!"

The story, in part, said:

"Directors and shareholders of Black Diamond No. 1 and Black Diamond No. 2 took a prominent part in the proceedings. Enterprising and energetic George E. Buck headed the procession as far as Okotoks. Thirty-two cars chartered by Black Diamond lined up at this point on either side of the road and gave the vice-regal party a vociferous reception. Horns and sirens, at a given signal, honked and shrieked while the occupants of the cars vigorously cheered, as the duke and his party passed through the lines.

"Immediately after the royal party cars passed, the Black Diamond cars took up the rear position, following to within a few hundred yards of the Dingman well. They took up a position on one of the hills overlooking the site and had a perfect view of the demonstration given at the well.

"The Black Diamond party then proceeded to their wells where luncheon was served. The wells were inspected. At No. 1 well the drill was pounding away.

"There is not the slightest question there is more oil in No. 1, than any other in Alberta and Black Diamond stock at the present price should not be overlooked.

"No. 2 well is under construction."

Buck failed to impress the B.C. investors, much less the Duke of Connaught.

After the incident a month later, with J.D. McGregor at the Carseland Dam cover-up, the duke no doubt went away shaking his head at the duplicity of some people in the wild and woolly Province of Alberta, trying to lay hoaxes on him to win his patronage. Buck, though, had more reason to seek the duke's patronage. He, after all, was of United Empire Loyalist stock:

The oil boom burst with the opening of the First World War, Aug. 5. The flow of money into oil stock was almost halted and hundreds of men, who were thrown out of work, flocked to the forces. Calgary, with its high concentration of British, turned all its thought to the

The Duke and Duchess of Connaught arriving at the 1912 Calgary Stampede.
Photo: Glenbow Archives, Calgary, Alberta.

war effort. Many packed their oil stock certificates in trunks or papered walls with them, then marched off to war.

In the fall and winter of 1914, Buck was in court to answer charges in a spate of civil suits, including one for $25,000 by Martin and Phillips, for drilling to 1,208 feet on Black Diamond No. 2. They had closed down the drill when Buck had consistently refused to furnish them with coal and water.

In one lawsuit, Buck failed to appear at an examination for discovery. Dec. 14, the sheriff was sent to bring him in from the drilling camp at Black Diamond. He found Buck had hired a police force to prevent him from entering the camp.

One Lawson, who claimed authority as an Alberta Provincial Police constable, and Harry C. Beatty threatened to place Bailiff D. McKay Murray under arrest — and they got away with it.

Buck's lawyer, A.A. McGillivray, won him a dismissal of all the lawsuits. The bilked shareholders were furious and called for a government commission of inquiry.

On June 22, 1915, Premier Alex Rutherford of Alberta, set up a one-man judicial committee under Judge Carpenter, with Frank Ford as counsel, to enquire into the bucket shops.

McGillivray put the commission out of business, on the constitutional ground, it had singled out Black Diamond for an inquisition. If the shareholders had a beef they had a remedy under the Companies

Act. The government had no business in interfering with Buck's civil rights. The fact the citizens had been fleeced in a most brazen manner, was held to be no business of the government. The citizens had had ample warning of what lay ahead of them in the press.

Buck lost no opportunity to gloat over the "democratic process" under which he was able to sway city aldermen, establish a newspaper and convert it to his own use, establish his own law and order at the Black Diamond well and thumb his nose at the Alberta government.

Attorney-General C.W. Cross couldn't take this insolence and set out to get Buck by charging him with fraud. The trial was delayed while Buck went on a short holiday, in Great Falls, Mont., but returned under his own steam with a great chance for grandstanding. The case was set down for trial Jan. 11, 1916.

But some time before Christmas, Buck manifested a stronger liking for the air of the great republic to the south. His trip there made him a sensational fugitive from justice in Canada — and an international incident almost blew up over it.

He fled to the U.S. with his bookkeeper, Hugh Miller. After extensive travels they ended up in Wichita, Kans., where they set up Miller Oil Syndicate and bought a big lease. He went under the assumed name of Joseph Barnes. He cut a handsome figure tooling around town in his big red car. Alberta Provincial Police, sent a "man wanted" circular with a reward of $1,000 to the U.S. Buck was spotted by the Wichita police chief. But since the police couldn't accept reward money, Chief Hayes conspired with two bounty hunters, McWain and Miller, to grab Buck in mid-April, 1916. Nicholson went to pick up Buck April 25, but the bounty hunters wouldn't produce him until they saw the $1,000 cash.

Although the cash was finally paid, the U.S. government refused to recognize the validity of the Alberta government documents presented to the police officials to extradite Buck. They didn't even recognize the Canadian Criminal Code.

They were barely cognizant of the existence of Canada or its great seal; assumed it was some sort of cold unsettled land up near the North Pole. As for Alberta, nobody had ever heard of it in Kansas. Poor Nicholson was forced to sit around in a hotel waiting 30 days for additional papers, mainly affidavits, then had to take them to Ottawa to be certified by the U.S. counsul, John Foster.

In the meantime Buck, accompanied by a bodyguard, was running around Wichita on bail attacking Attorney-General Cross. He proclaimed Cross would never extradite him — and he almost made that boast stick. His phenomenal luck held until July 17, when after serving a flurry of documents including writs of habeus corpus, his lawyer, George McGill, dropped out of the case. Buck had run out of money. His wife and five children had come to be with him.

Having run out of remedies before the court, Buck resorted to the old Doukhobor trick of presenting himself naked to the authorities. He was hustled aboard a train by Nicholson wearing only his trousers, with his suspenders dangling.

Back in Calgary he came to trial Oct. 26, 1916, and was sentenced to four years in jail for fraud.

Buck's lawyer McGillivray, appealed the case and Buck won it as the Crown had a weak argument. Some of the witnesses were not available, but the appeal was really won on the grounds Buck was not tried on the charge for which he was extradited from the U.S.

By that time, Cross had had enough of him and decided not to press the two other charges, if Buck agreed to leave Canada within 10 days and never return.

This Buck agreed to and went back to Wichita, where he was lost sight of by all the drilllers and others to whom his promises of great wealth came to nought. He died in 1944 near Spokane, Wash.

As a 1989 footnote: A new oil probe was set up without benefit of hearing evidence of the muddled and larcenous affairs of Buck.

Out of it came a government securities commission which was a watchdog to prevent companies from walking off with investors' money. Whether this was a good piece of legislation will depend in 1989, on the outcome of a one-man commission of enquiry into the bankruptcy of Donald Cormie's Principal Investment Group of Edmonton. In this case, more than $450 million invested by 67,000 Canadians, was allegedly siphoned off into other subsidiaries owned by Cormie. This was a monumental loss compared to that suffered by investors in Black Diamond.

Martin and Phillips lost a bundle on drilling of Black Diamond No. 2 and it nearly put them out of business.

The war had for all practical purposes ended the oil boom in the province. It also did in the Martin and Phillips business in Medicine Hat. They continued to keep the doors open after the war but business was at a low ebb as there was little activity in the oil patch.

Chapter 20

A New Start in Texas

Frosty had prepared himself for a move back to new oil patches in the U.S. However, before he left he had a final adventure in the Canadian North that reads like fiction more than fact.

He was engaged by a British syndicate in 1919, to make an oil reconnaissance of the north country. Going to London in November of that year, he established lines of credit with the Northern Trading Company, Revillon Freres, (a medium-sized fur trading company with headquarters in Athabasca town), and with the Hudson's Bay Company. With English geologists, Martin arrived back in Edmonton in March and at Athabasca prepared to take a party down the Athabaska River in boats and scows built during the winter.

The man who persuaded the British syndicate to take the flyer in Canada was A.F.A. Coyne. The centre of Coyne's activity was the little town, known in earlier times as Athabasca Landing but simply Athabasca, after it was incorporated in 1904. In 1912, it became the end of steel for Canadian Northern Railway branch 100 miles north of Edmonton.

At one stage in its development, the railway was projected north along the river through Pelican Rapids and House River to the tar sands at Fort McMurray.

Until the railway came the commerce of the whole Mackenzie River system passed through Athabasca. Goods were hauled by team along the Athabaska trail from Edmonton and transferred to barges and scows, for transportation along the river to Lake Athabaska and thence along the Slave River to Great Slave Lake and to the Mackenzie River. Athabasca was then the gateway to the north.

During the winter scows 50 feet long, 12 feet wide and 3 feet deep, were built along the river banks at Athabasca Landing. They would hold up to 10 tons. These flimsily-built scows were floated down the river in flotillas of 50 to 100 at a time, by large gangs of men. There was a sweep oar to guide each through numerous rapids. The flotillas tied up at night and the rivermen would pile onto the cook scow for grub.

Above: Freighting supplies on the Athabasca River.

Left: Frosty Martin on the Athabasca River. Note name of A.F.A. Coyne & Co. on freighter canoe.

Many of the scows were never brought back but were broken up for their lumber, at the new settlements downriver. Those which did come back upriver were "lined" or "tracked" by 15 men walking along the bank, pulling on a 500-foot rope line. A trip from McMurray required 3 weeks. Two hours trek and two hours rest was the routine. Most of the early oil well drilling equipment was taken downriver on the scows.

The biggest obstacle to navigation was Grand Rapids, where the scows had to be unloaded onto Grand Island, the freight hauled overland on a crude railway 1½ miles and reloaded on the scows which had been relined around the island.

The extension of the Canadian Northern from Athabasca to Fort McMurray to bypass the rapids never came off. Premier Arthur Sifton of Alberta, brother of Clifford Sifton, gave his blessing to construction of the Alberta and Great Waterways Railway which bypassed Athabasca through Lac La Biche. Around Athabasca old-timers bitterly said the A and GW, (now part of Canadian National Railways), was the primary means of servicing timber leases held by the Sifton family.

One of the passengers who paid $4 to take the train into Athabasca in the fall of 1912, was A.F.A. Coyne. He was a small, active man with black hair combed straight back, wore rimless spectacles and a small black mustache — a man who could talk the birds out of the trees.

The coach-class passengers rode in boxcars. Coyne always fond of luxury, rode first class in one of the cabooses.

Although he had a suite of offices in the Williamson Block in Edmonton, he operated for his forays along the river, out of a small wooden building on the bustling Athabasca waterfront. His name and that of his brother were painted on a large sign over the door. His brother was active in some of the enterprises, until a proxy fight resulted in them parting sworn enemies.

In the carrying out of his search for oil, he initially had some financing of his own and his family. The family in Scotland was well-to-do. He had been educated at George Watson School in Edinburgh, the equivelent of Eton. He knew how to write grammatically, beautifully and convincingly.

His search was spurred by the Turner Valley oil patch and the gas excitement in the Viking field. However, the Edmonton area oil promotions were not carried out with the same flamboyance and chicanery, which gave Calgary a black name for years.

The Athabasca Tar Sands at Fort McMurray contain a light crued in shade — oil which is still defying the oil patch to extract it cheaply, despite the expenditure of billions on extraction processes. The other kind of oil — and this is what Coyne ran into at House River — is a heavy, viscous, black asphaltic crude lying in an arc from Cold Lake to Peace River. There are three times more reserves of this goo than anything else in Alberta. The oil patch is still trying to figure out today, how to treat it so it can be profitably marketed.

Coyne realized Pelican Oil and Gas Company was onto a good thing when it made its attempt to finance the piping of natural gas to Edmonton from its House River well. A few years later he wrote:

"When it does happen — which it will, and soon — the oilfields of this great northland will stagger the world with their stupendousness." Right, but probably a century before its time.

He decided to grab a piece of the action by organizing a brokerage and mining firm, Northern Fiscal Agency Ltd. Secretary was Cecil T. M. Sapsford, advertising manager of The Edmonton Bulletin. The Bulletin at that time, was put out by a collection of oddballs who would promote anything anywhere.

He raised the money to float this company by travelling through the farming areas east of Edmonton, in particular the New Norway and Round Hill communities. The most extraordinary part of his money-raising campaign, was the way he stumped the countryside like an emperor. He travelled in a chauffeur-driven Cadillac.

"He put on a show that was really a classic," said an impressionable young farm boy of the time." Those dirt farmers and settlers were really impressed by his sales pitch. Nobody had any ready cash but somehow 3,550 of them dug out $5 and $10 bills from secret places and showered them on Coyne.

"He convinced a lot of farmers, including my dad, to give him postdated cheques against the time they sold their grain. That was his pitch — and they really ate it up — that oil would some day produce more wealth in one year than five grain crops. Gamble your farming profits with me and grow rich with the country."

That was 50 years before then Prime Minister Lester B. Pearson, adopted his idea and introduced the concept of the Canada Development Corporation. Coyne, however, never lived to see how the new wealth created annually by the oil patch is equal to five grain crops.

The farmers had oil fever and, in fact, many had previously made investments in the gas wells Tiny and Frosty brought in at Camrose and Viking.

One of the farmers who invested heavily was Falk A. Fergstad, a relatively wealthy and influential leader in the Round Hill district. He persuaded his brother, C.A. Fergstad, who was building inspector of Minneapolis, Minn., plus other neighbours and friends to invest $3,000 with Coyne. There were 194 shareholders all told.

Coal had made Fergstad rich. A gold nugget was found in the

crop of a Christmas turkey by an Edmontonian. (Few fowl sold in those days were eviscerated.) The turkey was traced back to the general store in Round Hill. Word of the find spread and next spring, hundreds of people started a minor gold rush as they took to all the rivers and streams in the area, with prospector's pans, along the streams and rivers where the turkey might have picked up the nugget.

Two of Fergstad's sons were panning gravel on a small stream which ran through the farm and they got a showing of something black in their pan. The "something black" came from a coal outcropping. Fergstad promptly opened a coal mine. It was the first mine in the area and he made a great deal of money from it as settlers and villagers from a wide area came there for their winter supply of fuel.

Later, when coal was found in larger quantities on the Battle River near Camrose, he decided to sell to Round Hill Collieries, so the mine might be developed along more economical lines. The terms of the sale were $5,000 cash for 40 acres of coal lands — a fabulous price at the time — and a royalty on every ton sold.

In the spring of 1915, Coyne made a deal with Great Northern Oil and Asphalt to continue the drilling of a well it had started at House River in 1914.

However, the company went insolvent with the outbreak of war. He used the funds collected from the farmers to make the deal. A note in Tiny's scribbler quoted Coyne as saying:

"The promotion was extraordinary because at that time, to speak of oil exploitation, was tantamount to sedition in Alberta owing to the cataclysm in Europe. Support for the Canadian troops was so intense it excluded support for almost everything else."

It was Sept. 15, 1916, before Coyne was able to get driller Robert Bradley to House River to start up Great Northern Oil and Asphalt's well again. When the drill got down to 415 feet with a showing of heavy black oil, Coyne had the rig shut down for the winter and went back to report to the farmer-shareholders in the Camrose area in October. He needed more money to continue drilling and where they had previously supported him with a gamble stake of $10, they began to write cheques for $500. Some of them postdated cheques for a couple of years ahead, the money to be paid when they sold their crops.

At the same time, he organized a new company — Northern Production Company — which went ahead and gradually acquired thousands of acres of lease and took over the shares of the bankrupt Great Northern Oil and Asphalt, to protect its shareholders from Great Northern's creditors.

The latter move projected him into a vicious battle complete with proxy fights, bitter rivalries, international cloak-and-dagger intrigue and court battles which turned his life into a boisterous turmoil that in the end, shattered his dream of a northern oil empire.

More than anything else Coyne was pleased to see the rural support he received:

"That money was given on a development spirit, in a spirit of faith in the country. It must have been given in a spirit of faith in me, because in 1915 conditions in agriculture and crop growing were not conducive to speculation. The uncertainties which had been brought about by the condition which existed in Europe, certainly gave an intuitive spirit to any man to beware of using surplus funds in speculative enterprises.

"I think it much to the credit of the province, that it can be said that this company represents an established confidence between citizens or rural and urban constituencies. It has been built entirely by the co-operative feeling of those two factors."

Acquiring oil lease holdings through one company then setting up a drilling company by public subscription — as Coyne did and George E. Buck did in Turner Valley — left the shareholders open to large risks because of a provision in the Canadian Petroleum Mining Act.

It was quite easy for any organizing company or body of individuals to agree to file on a certain area of land and pay the fees and therefore in fee simple, could become the owners of an immense area of oil lands. This agreement required that a certain amount of development work be carried out.

When the act was properly enforced, ordinary individual speculators were forced to do this work or drop the lease. It was easier for them to band together and form a company, assign their leases to the company and have the company undertake the development work.

To Coyne's way of thinking, the holding of thousands of acres of oil lease and the development of this natural resource, was the answer to reversing the flow of wealth out of Canada to support the war effort.

"If we keep importing more wealth than exporting it for a long period, the nation — like the individual — can become insolvent. There is only one way in which an adjustment can be effected and that is by developing the natural resources of this country: the immense deposits of tar sands, the petroleum deposits and so forth," Coyne wrote.

" . . . If we bring in a well at House River and it produces 200 barrels a day, the principal amount would be returned every year afterwards.

"Such a possible reward tempts us to part with our money in this business. We know that if our money is used for development work, then we will get a large return."

To some elements in the company this kind of thinking was seditious. They were having none of it. While Coyne was in New York during the winter of 1916-17, they tried to win control of the company from him.

What took him to New York, was an offer by German secret agents to keep his knowledge of the potential of the oil field away from their enemies, the English. The United States was not in the war at that time and German agents operated freely out of New York.

Through an intermediary named Schullman in Edmonton, he was given a large sum of money to keep his report of the potential of the field out of English hands. He accepted the money but duped the German, by making his findings known to the British anyway. The German agent whom he dealt with was naturally furious upon his discovery and set out to kill him. For three months the Coyne family were forced to hide out in New York at the home of a Jewish lawyer named Epstein. In the spring of 1917, when the United States entered the war, all known German spies were put under surveillance, thus removing the threat to the Coyne family. The night they arrived back in Edmonton the frustrated Schullman committed suicide. It was some time before this mode of ending his life was established. Police theorized it was murder — and who do you suppose was blamed?

On March 29, 1917, Northern Production Co. filed on 20,000 acres of petroleum leases surrounding the House River well. This precipitated a minor staking rush to the area, with Imperial Oil Limited acquiring 926,000 acres along the uncompleted A and GW Railway and the Tapley interests of California filing on 10,000 near Imperial'

Coyne said the result of his large leaseholding left Northern Production in "absolute control of many miles along the arch" and would "prevent repetition of the Calgary fiasco. Would a farmer go on the land and when he sees there is no security or possibility of obtaining the title, start to plow and put his efforts into it?"

When Coyne had obtained 20,000 acres of lease valued at $100 an acre, but no more progress had been made at the well by the summer of 1917 by Bradley, dissident shareholders were yapping at Coyne's heels. Their criticism became so loud he resorted to an old Edmonton Ad Club technique and took a group of representatives to inspect the well.

It became apparent Bradley was in trouble. On Sept. 18 it became necessary to shut down the work.

At an elaborately staged meeting in Edmonton in January, 1918, the delegation which visited the well for two days, helped Coyne overcome all opposition to proceeding with the well.

Following the meeting, Northern Production Company issued an annual report which was one of the most amazing — and by its own appraisal "comprehensive" — documents ever published in the oil patch in Canada. It was 90 pages, printed on slick 8½ x 11 paper and set mostly in 10-point type. Even now it would be a most valuable primer for the stock promoter, not only for oils but in any other form of industry. It was no shoddy piece of promotional bombast put together by a fast-buck artist. It was composed in the well-written prose of an educated man and covered everything from a history of the area, to an accounting of every cent spent. The last chapter is entitled: "My Fellowship With You."

Coyne's father, R.A.F.A. Coyne, and his grandfather were civil engineers, the latter having made a great deal of money as waterworks engineer for the City of Edinburgh.

Coyne was a man with a brilliant mind and brilliant ideas. He sought power and glory and was willing to go to any lengths to acquire greater status, even to the extent of making enemies and overriding all objections. He tackled problems with bustle and braggadocio, thoroughly preparing himself for the task at hand and not minding the consequences of his actions.

He was born in Scotland, to an upper class family, but he was willing to work hard. Coyne also respected the man who had to work with his hands to make a living.

Coyne was born to a moneyed class and had to have money whether — at times — the money belonged to him or not. Money meant status. However, what was accepted behaviour in the Old Country, was considered by people in northern Alberta to be out-and-out extravagance — a grand suite in the Macdonald Hotel in Edmonton, a plush suite of offices, a large river boat at Athabasca with a uniformed crew to sail dignitaries to the well, (it didn't make many trips — if any — because it was a keel boat rather than a flat-bottomed boat needed for Athabaska navigation.

Through his next door neighbour, P.S. MacKay of the Canadian Northern, he never had to go to the station to board a train but had the crews make special stops at 83rd St., a stone's throw from his house.

He operated in the grand manner. And yet in his later years he was called "a wild man — just like Hitler" and "counterfeit Coyne."

He never backed away from a good fight and showed the Scotch trait of stubbornness. He had a coterie of faithful followers who believed in his ability. He was proud of his talents as a promoter and for this, a segment of the business community hated him with vigor.

Despite his penchant for power and glory, he found the human need to be loved and admired. He gave this impression to the world.

His farmer-shareholders loved him. They had been slugging away at their homesteads alone for years and now they were being given recognition, by a man ostensibly leading their cause: development of their adopted country. They would have received no such recognition elsewhere.

Coyne said the American oil industry had become great because "Americans are good losers, therefore good speculators."

He predicted the oil patch would sustain the economy after the war.

These observations were prophetic, almost uncanny, in their accuracy. However, prophecy in regard to his own enterprise was as far off as any prophecy could ever be. His prophecy:

"We have no hesitation in stating, that within five years the company will be operating 1,000 wells on our leases."

At first, many businessmen thought Coyne was an awful four-flusher — but many changed their mind when they saw him in action. This prompted Sapsford to tell this story at the Edmonton meeting:

"There was considerable discussion in Minneapolis at one point about religion in the schools. It was decided to appoint a committee to thresh out the issue.

"Minneapolis is largely Swedish and Norwegian. They picked two good Norwegians and a Swede for the committee and told them to study the Bible and bring back a report. A report was made at which the chairman said:

"We ban thinking we won't teach the Bible in the schools."

Asked his reason, he said: "Well, we ban thinking it is a pretty smooth advertising game of St. Paul. We read a lot about St. Paul in the Bible — but not one word about Minneapolis. (Laughter.)

"You know, a good many people think that because Coyne has talked oil that there is a good bit of Coyne, (coin) there — but I believe that although Coyne has talked oil there is a good bit of real coin out there, and I think Coyne is going to show you where the coin is. (Cheers.)"

Drilling actively was carried out throughout 1918. It was continued in 1919 but came to an abrupt end one summer day. The end was witnessed by his son, J.A. Coyne of Edmonton;

"In the summer of 1919 I was fishing in the House River with a willow branch, when I was terrified by an explosion. The House River well had blown-up — and that was the end of my father's company, the Northern Production Co. Due to his extravagance, the shareholders would put no more money in the company to restore the damage — so his career in the West came to an end," he said.

Witnesses of the explosion have laid the blame on J.P. Scott, who was said to have walked into the rig with a burning cigarette at a time when gas was escaping. Why an experienced driller would pull a stunt like this, left a lot of question marks floating around. Some maintain he did it for revenge, as Coyne owed him money and he couldn't stomach Coyne's extravagant ways. At any rate he was badly burned in the explosion.

It would be more correct to say this was the beginning of the end for Coyne. He still had a couple of aces in the hole, with which he made several attempts to recoup his losses and exploit natural gas and oil in the Athabaska field.

Even before the drilling equipment was destroyed, Coyne had undertaken a campaign to acquire additional finances in London. He filed on another 169,000 acres with $25,000 in British finances in 1919. Two years later, Northern Production had enough capital to obtain 340 square miles of holdings on both sides of the Athabaska River.

Equipped with a parcel of leases and no drilling equipment and no way of raising further funds, he made his first attempt at recoupment in 1919 by giving a lecture before the London Institute of Science Technology.

In the 48 hours following the talk, he was assured of a sum of $200,000 for carrying on the work. He was asked by a company known as Anglo-Dominion Development Co. to prepare a geological report of the area following the lecture. This company was incorporated under the Companies Act of 1908, with head office at 6 Old Jewry, London. The company was so much impressed with his report it paid him $30,000 for it — a princely sum.

The report was turned over to Arthur Beeby-Thompson and Partners, a firm of petroleum engineers and geologists in London. After looking it over for six weeks, they recommended establishment of an oil subsidiary, Anglo-Dominion Petroleum Co. Ltd., and mounting an expedition to northern Alberta under its direction, to make an independent reconnaissance of the leases.

For his pioneering and development work in the world oil patch, Beeby-Thompson earned the soubriquet, "Father of the Oil Industry."

None other than Frosty Martin was hired as an engineer, to go with the expedition to determine the feasibility of moving in enough drilling equipment, for two or three test wells. Martin arranged river transportation for the spring of 1920. For this work he received $7,500 in salary and $5,000 expenses.

Coyne and Martin went to London in December, 1919, to make final arrangements with their British principals for the trip.

Martin's trip across the Atlantic was made on a ship which the passengers immediately dubbed the "Rollantic." Pictures he took show a great deal of rough water.

He was one of three Americans aboard the Rollantic and the British, (who made up most of the passenger list), didn't like the Americans in 1919 any better than they did in 1776. They were somewhat ostracized, along with two Chinese and a Brazilian coffee man, who could speak only one or two words of English he learned in shipboard poker games. The rest of the company called them the "foreign Gang."

As time went on, the foreign gang began seeing funny things aboard ship, many of them stories which made the British passengers the butt of amusement. Martin got the idea of writing down incidents. He wrote them in bulletin form and stuck them on the bulletin board at the head of the main companionway.

On board ship that took A.F.A. Coyne and party across ocean in search of British financing. November, 1912.

They were full of lively humour — but somehow were quickly ripped off and thrown overboard.

Beeby-Thompson sent a colleague, Ivan Ascanie Stigand, to Athabasca next spring — a man who proved he didn't have much stomach for the job: fraught with swamps and man-eating mosquitoes, boat upsets, boat break-downs, flooding of the Athabaska and delays in transit and the tiresome job of walking back.

Operating under these backwoods hardships and only doing a half-hearted reconnaissance, Stigand came back and, in October, 1920, issued a report saying he could see no commercial possibilities in the leases held by Coyne.

Coyne was furious. He made some wild charges against Stigand saying he had come under the influence of people at the Geological Survey of Canada, in Ottawa, who had placed faulty interpretations on the strata of the area. He was able to convince Anglo-Dominion Petroleum there were deficiences in the report. Another geologist named Campbell-Hunter was sent out in 1921 for another report.

The results of this survey were overshadowed by big trouble which Coyne got himself into at this time. He had some difficulty over his leases with government officials in Edmonton. He was enough of a rabble-rouser, that he talked a bunch of war veterans into arming themselves and taking over the government by force.

Those who remember this incident, (including his son), speak of it with awe and concurrence. It appeared to be the right thing to do, at the right time, in dealing with bureaucrats. However, because it was a blueprint for dealing with intractable civil servants, accounts of it have been kept well-hidden in court records and government archives and secret cabinet documents. There are, no doubt, people today who would be only too happy to dust off such a blueprint, to expedite their dealings with governments in Canada.

It is thus difficult to ascertain how far the plot had progressed. There are probably records of it in the Coyne family archives. The only reference Coyne himself made many years later, was that he was charged with seditious conspiracy. His lawyer walked out on him at the last minute — the same fate that befell George E. Buck, when he was fighting extradition to Canada from the United States.

He was convicted but, like Buck also, he was allowed to leave the country rather than serve a term in jail. This practice seemed to be more prevalent than generally realized. There is reason to suspect there was some dirty work afoot, to get rid of educated troublemakers.

In the interest of respectability, the family never had a monument erected at Athabasca for this illustrious ancestor. Perhaps it was because a member of another branch of the family, James Coyne, became a highly placed civil servant in Ottawa, the governor of the Bank of Canada.

Coyne left Canada in 1921 for a job in the geology department of Fort Wayne University, in the United States. The House River well was abandoned.

The question of how Coyne found it so easy and convenient to recruit an "army," may be answered by a concurrent adventure he carried out with the Town of Athabasca.

He secured an agreement with the town to supply the citizens with natural gas.

That Coyne would be given a franchise was almost a foregone conclusion. Before a vote of ratepayers was ever taken, he agreed to pay 10% of the net profits to a fund, to be divided among all returned soldiers and widows of soldiers and their dependents living within a 50-mile radius. They would have died for him after that magnanimous offer, the best they had had since they shucked their uniforms. And they almost got the chance to go to war again!

He also agreed to pay a royalty of 20% to the town if he struck oil in a well to be drilled within the town limits. He further agreed to supply gas for street lighting at 25 cents a light per month. When Coyne and Frosty Martin came back from their trip to London, Coyne learned the council had voted in favour of him getting his franchise at a meeting Dec. 22, 1919.

However, before work could get started, the town went bankrupt trying to pay off a $150,000 water and sewer debenture issued in 1913. The Alberta Public Utilities board refused the allow council to go ahead with installation of gas.

Coyne was in trouble with the same board at that time over some stock promotions, too. That was the end of that adventure for him.

After being given the bum's rush from Alberta, it would be assumed Coyne's bitterness toward the government remained with him for the rest of his life. But not so. In 1935, at the age of 62, he made one last attempt to resurrect his shattered oil patch empire on the Athabaska.

A year after William (Bible Bill) Aberhart was elected premier on the new Social Credit ticket in 1935, Coyne wrote him from London to offer to come to Alberta and organize an oil company, to exploit the great pool of oil he had come across 20 years previously. He said if the government would finance the venture to the tune of $75,000, he would take on the job of superintending drilling and all the profits from the wells would go into government coffers. He was careful to point out he was a firm believer in Social Credit. He was also 40 years ahead of his time; the governments began grabbing two-thirds of the oil patch profits in the 1970s.

Aberhart turned over Coyne's offer to a minor civil servant in the Alberta Department of Mines and Minerals for study. This official was Charles W. Dingman, a nephew of A.W. Dingman, the driller of the Turner Valley "discovery" well. He was not satisfied with Coyne's qualifications and, largely on that ground, he recommended Coyne's offer be turned down. It was done so quietly.

There are many who allege Aberhart made one of the biggest goofs of his political career in rejecting Coyne's offer, as oil revenues could have certainly paid more than one Socred "dividend" to Albertans of $25 a year he had promised.

Chapter 21

Martin and Decker Team Up

Frosty Martin left Alberta in 1921, the same year as A.F.A. Coyne. He had expected to do some drilling for Anglo-Dominion Petroleum, but this deal fell through. Times had been hard for International Supply Company, so hard that Maud Martin took a year in teachers' college to validate the certificate she held in Ohio — and went back to the classroom.

In the Medicine Hat business community, it was no disgrace the company went into receivership. It was merely the inability to hold on until the top of the oil patch boom-and-bust cycle was reached again.

Although Frosty was practically broke, he had enough confidence and know-how to leave for a job as lease man for Pearce Petroleum Company in Peabody, Kans., to start what became a five-year whirl of diversified activity in the booming oil patches of Kansas and Texas.

Frosty didn't leave Medicine Hat under a cloud; he just left. He had reached the age where his personality development had showed him to be a complex man, but he showed different qualities to different people. He was equally at ease in the mansions and offices of the mighty in London and, later, Washington, as he was in the tarpaper shacks of the rawboned Canadian frontier.

Frosty Martin had an inventive, fertile mind. He was a man of vision who thought big. He invariably did things with a flair. This combination of traits enabled him to cash in on a number of oil patch inventions by going into the marketing and manufacturing of them in a big way then and later.

An early Medicine Hat business acquaintance remembered him:

"He was well liked in this community. He was a man of good personal appearance. He had the ability to inspire confidence but he appeared to be the Get-Rich-Quick-Wallingford type." (Get-Rich-Quick-Wallingford was a post-First World War popular magazine fast-talking promoter but he always operated within the law. Wallingford always had a coterie of three or four hangers-on to assist with his schemes.)

J. Walter (Spud) Martin, his son:

"Dad's most distinguishing characteristic was his ability to strip away the dross from most problems and reach the heart of them quickly. He was a genius for winnowing an original conclusion from a mass of facts.

"He was also a soft touch for anyone with a hard-luck story. This may have contributed to his own financial hardship at times."

He was a big bluff Irishman of good bearing and a natural gift for blarney. He had a salty tongue which he knew how to use a friend or foe alike.

Above: Martin and Phillips machinery factory in Medicine Hat.

Right: Oil well machinery manufactured in Medicine Hat by company formed by W.R. Martin and A.P. Phillips.

Above: The Martins at home in Medicine Hat, circa 1909. Youngster is likely foster son, Harold Blythe.

Left: Frosty, Maude and Spud, circa 1919-20.

During his Long Beach days, he had a large house where he entertained acquaintances from important glamorous foreign potentates, to unpolished toolpushers and drillers from his early days in the East and Alberta. Arthur Beeby-Thompson recalled:

"On various occasions I was his honoured guest when he was indeed rich and was managing the harbour board's exploration program. I had placed many orders for his patented equipment. He was a remarkably able man and his inventions were famous in the industry . . ."

Beeby-Thompson adds a comment on the life and times in the United States during the Prohibition era:

"In 1930 . . . my stay in Long Beach confirmed my belief that so far as the wealthy classes were concerned Prohibition was a veritable curse, although it may have been a benefit to the working population.

"It was very hot in California. My friend, Frosty Martin, introduced me to the Pacific Club, at Long Beach and generously handed me the key of a room he reserved there and begged me to use it for the remainder of my stay. He laid emphasis on the fact that the contents of a cupboard in the room were at my disposal. I took advantage of the cool sea air and club amenities.

"I found the cupboard contained the widest range of alcoholic beverages, varied enough to satisfy the simplest and most fastidious tastes. In the days before it was made illegal to sell alcohol, all that a man like Frosty would have thought of providing would have been gin, whisky, brandy and possibly sherry. But so booze-conscious had Prohibition made folk that they now would have felt inhospitable if they hadn't had on hand every distillation of grain and grape to offer their guests.

"I was regarded as something of an oddity because I courteously declined bottles of Scotch, which the majority of callers brought with them; taking alcoholic refreshments while doing business in offices. This was cruelly hard on youngsters of weak resistance."

When he was able to afford it, (or maybe before) Frosty bought himself a $1,200 diamond ring.

Secretly, he did not consider the ring so much a token of affluence as of good luck. Even when he was down on his luck — a frequent occurrence in the oil drilling business — his impressive talisman seldon failed to influence his contacts, into thinking that he was a man of affluence. Good luck generally followed these contacts.

Keeping up an appearance of affluence was a part of the game in raw frontier country, where there was always a bit of suspicion of promotors who used the drill in mining ventures.

His struggle to affluence was a long one, coming well past age 50. Only a man with drive, a liking for hard work, inventiveness, ability, wit and charm to deal with all kinds of people, a gambling instinct, the brass and the dash imparted by wearing the expensive ring could have "made it."

When he left Medicine Hat in the early 1920s almost broke, his industry, action, travel and zest for life carried him swiftly away from that financial dead end, to another bigger fortune 15 years later. The ability to write off a loss, after years of work and tackle a new project with equanimity, added a Horatio Alger aura to his career.

Needless to say, the good luck ring played an influential role in this achievement. His old-time friends around Medicine Hat, used to say an indication of his financial status was whether or not he was wearing the ring. If he was wearing it, he was in the chips; if not it would likely be in hock somewhere as collateral for a loan.

By 1922, Frostyhad raised enough to buy a string of tools to drill a wildcat well in Bremond, Texas. It was only incidental when he decided to buy the string that he had no money.

That problem was resolved by borrowing a large flashy Cadillac, dressing up in his Sunday best and pulling up in style before an East Texas bank. Making an impressive entrance, Frosty had no trouble convincing the manager he was a big drilling contractor from Canada. With the help of his good luck ring he was able to negotiate an

The kickoff of a well at Bremond, Texas, with a huge 1922-style barbecue.

unsecured loan in a matter of minutes — and was in business again as a contractor for Clark No. 1 at Bremond!

Frosty's new start in the U.S. found him entering a field of activity, where there was more money to be made: that of manufacturing improved drilling equipment.

Although he was a dyed-in-the-wool standard tool driller, he had the foresight to see the days of this drill would diminish, as the rotary outfits were improved and could be used to drill the deeper wells required.

On every job he was on he was an innovator. One of the devices which he helped perfect was a furnace for heating babbitt, to make guides for sucker rods.

The sucker rods were used to activate oil well pumps. The babbitt guides served to centre the rods inside the well casing.

He and another driller, John Hoosier, set up a small company to

Left: Sucker rods.

Below: This unlikely looking contraption was invented to join sucker rods together with babbit to pump oil through the rods.

specialize in running the babbitt melting outfit at Wichita Falls, Texas. Hoosier wanted him to become a permanent company employee but Frosty was having none of that. His instinct for working for himself was too strong. Spud Martin remembers:

"I witnessed the way he and Hoosier parted. Mother and I had moved to Cypress, Calif., 14 miles east of Long Beach, and were there two years before dad followed us. I went back to Wichita Falls to visit him one summer vacation.

"Nothing Hoosier could say or do could sway dad from leaving. In a magnificent gesture of good will Hoosier gave him a brand-new Cadillac and wished him well. I was very much impressed by that car."

In 1925, Frosty headed for Long Beach and found a job in the design field, with Walter Loomis of the Loomis Oil Well Control Company. He had not worked for Loomis long when he suggested the idea for a weight indicator. The company spent considerable time and money on this invention but, as is usual with the first models of many new machines, it was not too successful. In light of today's knowledge of hydraulics, the original Martin design did not function because of packing friction leaking. Frosty was naturally somewhat disappointed, because the industry was looking for just such an invention. He had been thinking about it many years. The concept was simple but the practical application eluded the company.

Frosty surrounded by a forest of derricks at Signal Hill, near Long Beach, California, circa 1929-30.

Broadly here is the idea of the weight indicator:

By the time a rotary drilled well reaches a depth of, say, 4,000 feet there are many tons of weight on the drill stem, if the weight of that length of pipe is all let down at once. There would be enough weight that the stem might twist off, if it hit a piece of tricky rock. That would mean pulling the pipe and doing a fishing job to recover the bit. On the other hand, if too little weight were put on a drill stem the drill wouldn't make progress.

The weight indicator told the driller how much weight was on the bit and if there was too much, some of it could be lifted and hung on the rig's crown block instead.

It was not until Mark Haynes, one of the young engineers employed by the company, suggested the diaphram type of deflection pressure transformer, in which the weight in a kink in a cable was registered on an ordinary steam gauge, that the weight indicator business began to take hold.

The invention was so simple — but necessary — that there actually was a potential sale to every rotary driller in the world. Today few, if any, rotary drillers, would start a hole without a weight indicator.

Some of Frosty's friends in Medicine Hat still avow he and Tiny Phillips were both involved in the invention of the weight indicator. This was unlikely, since no rotary equipment was being used in Alberta at that time and there was no need for the equipment here. Further, the original was nothing like the model which was offered to the industry in 1926. Other friends maintain he had turned out his first working model in the International Supply Company shops, and that it had been stolen. This is an unlikely occurence, also. Whatever the truth, it is an inescapable fact the weight indicator business did not really begin to take hold, until the model with the Hayne's diaphragm was produced.

Then the weight indicator began to sell like mad. The part Frosty Martin played in the development of this valuable instrument for rotary drillers enabled him, in 1926, to persuade Loomis to set up a separate corporation to carry out its manufacture, called Martin-Loomis Corporation. Frosty acquired one-quarter of the stock.

The fledgling company made rapid progress for the first two years. Then some fundamental disagreements shaped up. Loomis had a tendency to be the playboy type and did not pay as much attention to business details as Frosty would have liked. Such a situation could have become intolerable. The impasse was resolved by the entrance of a third party.

Chapter 22

Frosty the Flying Salesman

In 1927, Elmer L. Decker came to work for Loomis as a salesman. In 1928, Loomis decided to sell the weight indicator subsidiary. He sold it to Martin and Decker who, in turn, moved to a small factory.

Martin and Decker had common backgrounds as salesmen. The force that impelled them to set up their own company, was the desire to be in business for themselves rather than have someone else skim the cream off the profits.

Martin said years later: "I was a little different from the average nutty inventor. I decided I was going to cash in on every cent possible for anything I invented for the oil patch, by manufacturing the gadgets and merchandising them."

He had one advantage over "Deck" Decker. He was a born fund raiser. He was able to raise enough to acquire two-thirds of the stock in the new company. They acquired a new property and built a small modern plant; and changed the name to Martin-Decker Corporation.

In addition, it began manufacturing companion drilling control units and several other Martin innovations: recording and pump gauges, recording torque gauges, rotary table tachometers, pump gauges, rate of penetration records, check valves.

In the construction of Boulder Dam in Colorado, a tensiometer invented by Frosty was used on the high-line cables. During a trip to the dam, in 1935, in connection with maintenance on the instrument, Frosty found the chief engineer was none other than A.H. (Gus) Ayers, whom he had met years before as a resident engineer for the Southern Alberta Land Company. It was a happy reunion full of Canadian reminiscences.

It was nearly a quarter of a century since the two had undergone their Canadian "apprenticeship," a time of accomplishment carried out under fairly primitive conditions. America had made great strides in mechanization, mainly because of cheap petroleum available to power the engines.

For instance, in 1907, there were no road bridges across the South Saskatchewan River in the Medicine Hat area. Tiny and Frosty had a drill rig, there but no way of moving it 40 miles directly to J.D. McGregor's Home Ranch near Ronalane. The only means was having the CPR haul it to Suffield and then transferring it to wagons.

However, they got around the river barrier by moving the drilling on the river from Medicine hat, on a paddlewheel steamer.

The surveyors on the immense SAL irrigation project, where Ayers was employed as a resident engineer at the Carseland dam, travelled mostly by horse and buggy. This meant engineers and surveyors in the field probably saw the chief engineer once in a season and if they saw the division engineer more than once, they were lucky.

It took three days for a survey party to move from Ronalane to the south end of Lake McGregor, the chief reservoir of the SAL. This was a 22-mile-long lake, of 360 acre-feet, created by damming two ends of a valley. The intake was 40 miles from the Carseland dam.

The office and staff at the Martin-Loomis Corp. at 2877 Willow Street in Long Beach. Elmer Decker is third man from left. Frosty Martin in white shirt with bow tie.

This historic 1939 photo shows Frosty Martin, left and E.L. Decker, centre, with their first company aircraft. Other man unidentified.

There were no telephone lines between Carseland and Medicine Hat.

It was fortunate the field staff and the resident and consulting engineers didn't see much of each other, as it saved a number of squabbles.

The first resident chief consulting engineer was an Englishman brought out of retirement from Sidney, B.C. He was R.G. Kennedy and he figured the company had saddled him with a bunch of inexperienced "colonials." The colonials included Americans who were well trained and capable, but most were junior engineers who were pitchforked into senior jobs by SAL.

These engineers no doubt resented Kennedy's cavalier attitude and some of his critical remarks, about their abilities and quality of their work. But there was nobody else available. Many gained fabulous hands on experience in Canada in a hurry on this job, which would have taken them years to achieve in the U.S. And they made some mistakes.

Ayers opinion was: "Kennedy was one man nobody could please, no matter how much one did for him. His engineering background was sound, but he would brook no radical ideas from younger men. His experience had been gained largely in India, where quite different sets of values and methods were in practice."

Had it not been for the persistence of some American engineers, the diversion and spill dams at Carseland would have been built of

Caption on back of original photo as printed by Spud Martin, reads: "This was one of tension indicators invented by W.R. "Frosty" Martin as used on a high line during construction of Boulder Dam in Nevada. Mr. Gus Ayers was the Chief Engineer for the "Six Companies" who constructed the dam. Man at right is Harold J. Blythe who was raised by the Martins and who I considered my brother."

bricks; as well as the two-mile tunnel at the outlet from Lake McGregor, the system's principal reservoir.

Kennedy had an obsession with bricks. During his tour as chief irrigation engineer of the State of Punjab, labour and clay were cheap. Reinforced steel was too costly. He was all for setting up a brick factory on the Carseland site and using that material.

Finally, the engineers took up a collection and sent one of their number to Calgary, to buy a standard text on reinforced concrete and they placed it in a conspicuous place, in Kennedy's quarters. No further mention was made of a brick dam. His overbearing manner on the job didn't create the esprit de corps needed, for successful pursuance of the project.

Although thwarted in the construction of the Carseland headworks, Kennedy's obsession for brick construction manifested itself again, for the tunnel to carry the canal along a sidehill 150 feet above the Little Bow River, where it emerged from Lake McGregor. Tenders actually went out for it. Later he was prepared to cancel the contract and use a make-do wooden flume, in the most dangerous area of slippage, along the sidehill. His reason for brick construction was that if made of concrete, the thickness would have to be greater and there is always the possibility of a weak spot, much more so than brick.

The prospects of obtaining cheap brick were good, because there was a natural gas line passing within 30 miles of the job site, (i.e., the line from the Bow Island well to Calgary). A small line could be brought to the construction site and provide heating for the brick kilns.

Gravel for concrete is hard to get in this country and although the CPR is building a rail line through the area which would allow for a saving in transport charges on cement, it may not reach here in time, Kennedy reasonsed.

No doubt Kennedy felt his stand was vindicated later on, when reinforced concrete proved to be no match for the summer flood of the Bow River in 1912 — a flood which caused the intake to collapse and was the first step in shutting down the project.

Water was carried from the Bow at Carseland, by a canal, to Lake McGregor. However, five miles from Carseland it was necessary to excavate a "big cut" 1¾ miles long and 64 feet deep, containing 1.5 million cubic yards of material. The construction contract was let to J.D. McArthur, a Winnipeg railway contractor, who indeed built a small

The Southern Alberta Land Company Dam, at Carseland. Constructed to raise river level roughly 100 feet to direct water into canal and on to the McGregor lease at Ronalane, near Medicine Hat.

railway, complete with three dinky engines and tram cars, to haul the material away from the face. He later built the Alberta and Great Waterways Railway in northern Alberta.

The first of the dinky engines was sent to Gleichen on the CPR, where it was transferred to wagons for a 28-mile trip across the dusty prairie. To quench their thirst before the dry trip, the crew adjourned for a spell at a hotel in Gleichen. They all roared out and, hooking up a 12-horse hitch, proceeded to the first big bend outside of town and promptly upset the load. It took a week to reload the engine.

The great shovels to tackle the cut were moved from the railway to the job site, by laying tracks ahead of them, moving them to the end of steel, then tearing up the track and laying it ahead of them again.

It took three years to remove the earth from the big cut. Work didn't go as it had been planned. George G. Anderson, an engineer formerly with the U.S. Reclamation Service, was consulting engineer. His test borings had not indicated the true nature of the soil with which he was dealing. It was only when McArthur's big shovels were well into construction, that it was discovered there was gumbo underneath the sand and gravel overburden. Alberta gumbo is the most treacherous soil in the world, for contractors to work with. It is usually water-bearing and subject to slides.

Anderson had changed the specifications on the cutbank and ordered them to be finished steeper than first drawn: almost vertical. This, he avowed, would do away with snow gathering on the banks in winter, then thawing, softening the material and causing slides. It wasn't until they were well into the job, the slides started to occur — and he had to go back and do it over to the original specifications. He had not taken into consideration, that summer rains would cause sloughing of the steep slopes; also that watery gumbo began slipping.

One big slide occurred behind one of the shovels and shut the job down for a month, until another shovel could be brought onto the site to dig it out.

McArthur was heard to grumble that he had made plenty on his contracts on the canal and embankments but he lost it all on the big cut and was nearly ruined.

Another engineering failing that plagued McArthur was lack of a contingency fund. Ayers knew all about this when he was brought back to the project for the second time, to get the project operative again, in 1913, after the intake collapse at Carseland. He found it necessary to have McArthur come in and rehabilitate ditching contracts done by subcontractors.

Some of the subcontractors had gone broke, walked off the job, abandoned their contracts and proved unreliable. Some of their work, which had lain dormant for several years, had been ravaged by the elements. McArthur was obligated to have it done over. However, some had to be done on a contingency basis but SAL did not have such a fund.

At one point McArthur had $90,000 on his hands from the contractors, who had removed 11 million cubic yards of earth to install the various works with horse-drawn scrapers and fresnoes.*

He had no definite arrangement as to payment for slides, either in writing or verbally, but the chief engineer gave him to understand, that in the final settlement they would go into the matter and pay him what was just and fair. The engineering staff was worried McArthur would get so discouraged he would abandon the work.

Another quirk of nature to trap the unwary was the nature of the Bow River itself. Its flow is about 24,000 cubic feet a second at Carseland, in the spring freshet. But in addition to the spring run-off, there is usually a bigger flood in July or August, when the meltwater from the glaciers in the Rocky Mountains comes coursing down.

This was the reason for the intake structure collapsing — the accident that caused McGregor's dismissal as manager of the SAL. Because the dams were not anchored, the force of the river was so great water began undermining the outlet and sluice gates.

In attempting to make repairs, a diver was killed. The unfortunate Englishman had gone down to position some piles and somehow wedged his foot under some cribbing. Although repeated attempts were made to rescue him all failed. In the end, 16 men frantically pulling on a rope to try to dislodge him, pulled the helmet off his diving gear.

One of the discussions by Martin and Ayers at their meeting at Boulder dam was about Cora Hind's foray into the public relations field. She was agricultural editor of the Winnipeg Free Press, who gained fame for her uncanny yield estimates of the Prairie wheat crop before it was harvested. She made her estimates, by travelling through the Prairie Provinces, personally inspecting hundreds of fields of ripening wheat. This was before the trade depended upon the prairie wheat pools , or the Canadian Wheat Board to do the job on a more scientific basis. Her estimates resulted in setting the prices at which growers could expect to be paid, when they delivered their crops.

---

* dirt scrapers

*E. Cora Hind became internationally
famous as a journalist, lecturer and
agricultural authority. Photo:
Glenbow Archives, Calgary, Alberta.*

Before her trip around the Prairies to make her 1912 crop estimate, Miss Hind paid a visit to the SAL and produced an illustrated 5x7-inch souvenir booklet for J.D. McGregor entitled "The Big Ditch." It is now a collector's item.

It was as fine a piece of commercial puffery as was ever written by any farm writer, with a reputation for objectivity. Those in the know, like Martin and Ayers, suppressed a chuckle or two when they read it. However, she might have been excused on several counts for, in this incursion into the engineering and construction field, she was writing on commission and wrote only what was evident on the surface. It has been speculated that McGregor and his chief project engineer, Arthur M. Grace, formerly of the Alberta Railroad and Irrigation Company, did not have any over-all conception of how bad things had gone awry. It was another speculation they wished to keep the shareholders from knowing.

In the flowery and discursive style of her day, Miss Hind proceeded with her work in the style of a homily, in which she likened the watering of the immense dry tract along the Bow River in southern Alberta, as analogous to the scriptural passage:

"Give me a blessing. Thous hast given me a southland, give me also springs of water; and he gave her the upper and nether springs."

In a way, the engineering staff was working from a position of blindness, as they did not know in advance how much water they were expected to deliver: in other words, how many acres of annual irrigation were to be done.

From an engineering standpoint, it was almost inconceivable that they would commence the construction of a works on as large a scale as the Southern Alberta Land Company did, without any idea of what capacity the key structures were expected to deliver. But apparently that is what happened, Ayers concluded.

A factor that worked against the SAL being successful from a financial standpoint was the demand by the government that all irrigation works be installed before a single settler was allowed on the huge tract. Had the company been able to complete small segments and throw them open as the project progressed, some revenue would have started to roll in. This cash could have been used to provide the necessary englargements or alterations. As it was, this cost was thrown back on the shareholders in England and they started rebelling. The government irrigation stipulation also put pressure on the engineering staff to rush the work and corners were cut.

One other point the pair discussed at the Boulder Dam reunion was the fact that, although J.D. McGregor was a man of vision, he didn't have the ability to attract enough loyal men around him like his old political boss, Clifford Sifton.

Loyalty isn't one of the virtues of a frontier-style economy in which the future appears uncertain and unstable. Many of the men he hired were just there to make a quick stake and leave for other parts. This type of economy and the fact the project was spread out over a long distance from the source of money and administrative control, left the operation open to graft of all kinds. McGregor didn't have the ability to control the graft. All these factors sent the works nearly 10 times over budget.

What started out to cost $1 million had now required $10 million.

Sir Frederick Williams-Taylor, president of the Bank of Montreal made an extortive pitch to the Robert Borden government, to bail out the company, lest Canada's credit rating on the world scene would be adversely affected if the project went into receivership and 5,000 influential English capitalists lost their money. He also suggested such a possibility could have an effect on immigration to Western Canada.

Of course, the company was into the bank for a great deal of money and Sir Frederick had a vested interest in getting government protection.

In 1914, Finance Minister Thomas White recommended to the government it refuse all SAL help. His political hide was only saved by the outbreak of the war — a time when hundreds of millions of dollars sprang loose from nowhere and all other problems paled into insignificance.

Borden, the politician, relented and gave SAL a refund of $380,000, the amount paid by the company for the purchase of the tract to be irrigated. He agreed to striking out the clause in the agreement stating that, one acre out of every four sold must be irrigated. Two factors influenced his decision:

1. several thousand jobs would be lost if the project were shut down.

2. Irrigation had been classed as a works for the general advantage of Canada.

One of the sidelights of this project which fascinated Martin and Ayers was the "Sifton option." McGregor had gone to his old friend, Clifford Sifton, for his help in bailing him out of some of the financial difficulties SAL had got into. He sought out Sifton in the summer of 1912, just before he was given the axe.

Sifton was a silent partner in the Grand Forks Cattle Company, which McGregor had used to acquire a federal government grazing lease which was assigned to SAL. The lease was approved by Sifton as minister of the interior. During Sifton's inspection trips of government projects in the Canadian West, he had a private railway car made available to him. When this car was "set off" at the Bow Island siding, this was a signal that a board meeting of the Grand Forks Cattle Company was being held at the Home Ranch.

In 1912, when Sifton was no longer in government, he went to see McGregor for advice on buying a large block of land near Winnipeg and developing it for market gardening. He intended to bring in settlers from Europe, who were used to working small holdings of 10 to 40 acres.

McGregor was able to convince him the SAL would be much better adapted to that kind of agriculture than the Winnipeg district and the produce could be put on the market just as quickly as if it was brought to Winnipeg from the farms by teams. Two other advantages were that the SAL was closer to the Calgary market and the towns in between and that the season was earlier than Winnipeg.

The result was that Sifton signed an agreement to buy 25,000 acres in the Vauxhall-Grantham area, with an option to buy 50,000 more. An agreement was reached that when the water started running, in 1913, through SAL canals, his land would be the first unit to be irrigated. The Sifton option was analogous to those SAL had signed with Canadian Wheat Lands Ltd. and the Alberta Land Company to deliver water.

With this magnificent piece of salesmanship and an option in his pocket, McGregor got some of the shareholders' heat off himself for the poor engineering that was costing them money.

With his son, John, Sifton planned to set up a land settlement company called the Alfalfa Land Company and retail irrigated land for $100 an acre.

Of course, when the SAL could not deliver water to Sifton, in 1913, because of the Carseland intake collapse, the option was cancelled.

However, he came back and signed a new option for a reduced acregage. This agreement carried over to the reorganizing of SAL with government assistance, in 1917, as the Canada Land and Irrigation Company. Canadian Wheat Lands Limited and Alberta Land Company were included in the amalgamation.

By 1920, when it didn't seem that the company was going anywhere fast, Sifton dropped the option and asked for his $20,000 back. The reason for Sifton's withdrawal was because of an argument, over whether he or the company was obligated to construct the irrigation works within his option. He didn't think this work was up to him.

Chapter 23

The Long Beach Harbour Development

W*hen Frosty Martin* and Gus Ayers ended their visit to Boulder Dam in 1936, it was back to the serious business of making, applying and servicing Frosty's cable tensiometer.

This instrument was used that year also, when the wreckage of a Standard-Oil Company airplane — in which three people lost their lives — was lifted from the waters of Great Salt Lake in Utah. It was used to aid in preventing additional damage to the plane's frame, as the company was desirous of recovering the plane without more damage.

Unfortunately, the directions for its use were lost. The company did not want to wait for another set of instructions by mail. Therefore it asked Frosty, who had patented the device two years previously, to wire a set of instructions. The message was 800 words.

The tensiometer was clamped to a cable to show how much tension was being exerted. This had the effect of preventing a crew from breaking a cable, or damaging the object to which the cable was attached.

The largest indicator made by Martin-Decker, weighed 40 pounds and the capacity was 260,000 pounds on a $2\frac{1}{8}$-inch cable. In addition to the uses mentioned, it was used on the Golden Gate Bridge at San Francisco for cable equalizing.

Frosty held original patents on 44 instrument inventions and improvements when he finished his career with Martin-Decker.

One of his biggest coups was improving the mud pump with the recording gauge.

In rotary drilling, high-pressure pumps are required to pump special heavy mud into the drill holes, to keep the hole from caving in during pulling of pipe to change bits. The mud is also used to close off water and sand as the hole is drilled. The mud is pushed in at pressures of 15,000 to 20,000 pounds per square inch. It will keep

Frosty Martin the inventor, with models of his weight indicators. Though the photo is from the 1950's, it is believed possible that Martin's earliest weight indicators were built many years previous in Medicine Hat.

the hole from filling up with water, by plugging the crevices in the formation.

Although these pumps are a great boon to rotary drillers, it takes a great deal of know-how to handle them. At times the high-pressure pumps failed and the mud became caked solidly in the hole and couldn't be drilled out. It is esential that a recording gauge be used to know accurately at all times, what is happening to the mud.

Although they were accurate and sensitive instruments, they had to be extremely rugged to withstand vibration and battering of drill rigs. Most of them were portable and could be hauled around in the back seat of a car and hooked to almost any rotary rig without alterations to the rig. All over the world, oil fields drillers could point to weight indicators in daily service for as long as 10, 15, 20 years.

Tiny Phillips acted as the company's Canadian representative for over 20 years. He made repairs to weight indicators in the basement of his Calgary home.

Some time after the 1947 discovery of oil at Leduc set off Canada's biggest oil boom Martin-Decker set up a branch office at Edmonton to handle the business.

The company made money because the instruments were applicable not only in the oil industry, but were used on ships, in shipyards, on dredges, derrick hoists, floating hoists, on suspension bridges, in the aeronautical field and in the lumbering industry. The U.S. Navy adapted weight indicators for use on its cranes.

The export trade made up a great deal of the company's business. Both Martin and Decker made extensive selling trips abroad. By 1943, Frosty had made seven world tours of oil production centres. Each trip averaged about 48,000 miles.

Both men were members of the Nomads, an organization made up of men who have travelled in foreign lands for the oil field supply industry. Decker was the founder of Nomads and was its first national president. Frosty was a charter member.

Besides sales trips, the firm exported by direct shipments. Much of its success here was that, contrary to the usual procedure in selling foreign customers, Martin-Decker shipped on open account.

"We never lost a penny," said Frosty. "There is no mystery about foreign trade. It's just like going across the street to sell to one of your neighbors. It just requires a little more paper work, that's all."

Many foreign visitors were attracted to the plant because of its location in the fabulous Signal Hill area of Long Beach.

Frosty made one of the trips around the world in 1937. He was accompanied by Maud and Spud. This was a memorable trip for Spud, not so much because it was his first globe-girdling tour, but because 9,000 miles of it was made by air. At that time, Spud was in the airplane business. He told how it all came about:

"The first ride I ever had in a plane was when I was seven years old. It was at the Medicine Hat fairgrounds in 1919. A group of barnstorming pilots were taking people for flips and Dad paid for a ride for me. Dad had flown in some of the early aircraft in Alberta and, with the long distances to be covered in this big country, realized that aviation had a great potential. He wanted me to develop a feeling for the airplane — and decided to start me off young.

"I thought the 15-minute flight was wonderful. Although I could barely see over the edge of the cockpit of that surplus First World War plane, I never forgot it. I never forgot the pilot either. He was Freddie McCall of Calgary, one of the greatest fighter pilots Canada produced in the First World War."

McCall, along with two other wartime Royal Flying Corps buddies, Charles Beeching and W.R. (Wop) May, had continued stunt flying, selling rides and developing commercial aviation in the West after

Barnstorming pilots delighted western Canadians with aviation acrobatics.

their military days were over. These fliers inspired a great many hero-worshippers to take to the air and become air-minded.

Frosty Martin was very quick to recognize the possibilities of the airplane in his type of business. Martin-Decker became one of the first companies to own its own aircraft and he was among the pioneer flying executives of the United States. The first plane was a SM8A Stinson high-winged cabin monoplane, appropriately called The Indicator. It wasn't long before other businessmen were taking a good hard look at this speedy method of transportation.

In the meantime, Spud had learned to fly in his last year of high school at Anaheim, under Bob Blair. In the sumer of 1930, Spud and Blair piloted The Indicator to Medicine Hat, crossing the border at Great Falls, Mont., with Frosty along for the ride.

The visit was a sensation to Frosty's friends in the 'Hat, as the return of any affluent business man who had left town broke nine years before would be.

Jack Burton, a 'Hat laundry man, recalled: "We all thought Frosty was a great man to know. I know there was a great deal of admiration around our dinner table, for anyone who could reach his pinnacle of success and own a plane. There was much excitement and talk about him in town, as he sent many of his friends up for spins in the craft. He arranged for my mother and me to go up. It was our first plane flight."

The occasion of the Medicine Hat trip was a memorable one for

Barnstorming planes at Skiff. A young Spud Martin caught the flying bug here and went on to a distinguished career in aviation.

Spud, because of a flight they made to a rodeo "at either Skiff or Vauxhall, I forget now. Anyway, the plane hit a gopher hole upon landing and broke the tailwheel.

"We were stuck there two days until we could arrange for a welder from a garage to come out and repair the wheel. There were several other planes at that particular rodeo. One hapless pilot went home minus his plane. He had cracked a strut on that rough landing field. When the welder attempted to repair it, he set the plane afire and it burned up."

Spud Martin's interest in flying was a permanent one — so deep that Frosty reluctantly came to the realization, his son would never follow in his footsteps in the oil patch. In 1943, demand for planes became so pressing that Frosty Martin organized a company to distribute, assemble and maintain light planes. It was located at the municipal airport. Called Aircraft Associates, the company was nominally for Spud's benefit, although the management at first was in the hands of Harvey Martin, a pilot and flying instructor at Long Beach airport, but no relation. Before the Second World War, the company had the distinction of being the largest distributor of light aircraft in the United States. The enthusism of father and son for flying, helped make Long Beach as aviation-conscious as any city in the United States. For a time Frosty headed the city's aviation committee and was a member of the Aviation Breakfast Club, which sponsored social fly-ins.

Frosty Martin never travelled any other way when he could fly, once flying became an established business in the United States. Early in April, 1939, he was in Houston, Texas, where he had been re-elected an Oil World Exposition director. The Long Beach Independent records he left Houston by plane at 8.40 p.m. and, after travelling in five different planes, arrived home the next day at 10 a.m.

Meanwhile, Spud had enrolled at the Universty of Southern California, where he took a science course, majoring in commercial aviation. He did not drop his flying, but became a member of the flying team which competed with other colleges.

In 1937, upon graduating with his degree, Spud was ready to have a look at the world with his parents. His plans fitted in with those of Frosty, who combined sales trips to the oil centres, along with inspecting airport and passenger facilities in the foreign cities they visited.

"There were few oil fields we did not visit on that trip," said Spud. "Sales were made in all major oil-producing countries except Russia and China. The Russians, who were producing extensively in the Baku oil fields, copied the weight indicator but there was nothing the company could do to collect inventor's royalties."

Although Maud did much of her travelling on the 1937 trip by train or boat, (she flew only 600 miles), Frosty and Spud made more miles by air than they did by boat. Surprisingly, they found Singapore was one of the chief aviation centres of the Far East. While Maud stayed there, the two men kited to different fields — where Standard and Shell oil companies were engaged in exploration and drilling — to make sales of equipment.

The travellers had plenty of stories to tell upon their return. One flight was made in an old Fokker land plane over 60 miles of open water. Another jaunt was 1,100 miles over jungle. On an air ride of 1,000 miles over the ocean and jungle to Batavia, Java, they encountered the ultimate in bad flying weather. Frosty was to describe it as "zero, zero, zero." They were half an hour finding enough holes in the clouds, to go down to the airport after locating Batavia.

One of Frosty's favourite yarns about their stay in Japan, concerned the time he and Spud dropped into a bar. They noted a wide variety of well-known brands of Scotch, bourbon and other types of firewater were available. They commented on this to the Japanese bartender. He replied:

"Oh yes, all brands — and all made right here in Japan."

Spud martin assumed the vice-presidency of Aircraft Associates following the trip. With the approaching entry of the United States into the Second World War, he became director of youth flight training courses under the national defence program for the Long Beach area. To gain nation-wide publicity for the program in July, 1940, Martin took 14 college youths who had graduated from the course to Lock Haven, Pa., to pilot back for Aircraft Associates, 14 new Piper Cub planes.

This was the first time any such group flight was undertaken with fledgling pilots.

Later Spud joined the U.S. Army Air Forces ferry command flying bombers to Allied forces throughout the world. The United States government took over the company, just as the government took over his father's company in Medicine Hat, during the First World War. Following the war he assumed presidency of Aircraft Associates and it became a company handling airplane maintenance and repairs and specialized in converting surplus military planes to civilian use.

Chapter 24

Frosty Martin the Innovator

Although Frosty Martin took a keen interest in political and civic matters and was a member of the Republican Party, he had a hearty dislike of party politics. He never ran for office — but helped to elect others.

Paradoxically, it was an involvement with some of his Republican cronies which resulted in his appointment to the Long Beach Board of Harbour Commissioners in September, 1939.

Up to 1936, Long Beach had the image of a small, sleepy southern California seaside tourist resort — little different than many other similar towns in the state. Spasmodic amounts of private and municipal funds had been spent trying to improve the harbour, but time and again the crashing Pacific Ocean surf and silt-laden rivers filled up the channels, that had been dredged in the mud flats.

The turning point in 1936 came, when oil was discovered in the Wilmington field north of Long Beach and the pool extended under Long Beach harbour. After East Texas, Wilmington was the second-largest producing field in the U.S. Production reached a billion barrels by 1964. Oil drilling, which had previously been banned in the city, was opened up with the prospect of millions in oil royalties being made available to the harbour commissioners, for the long-sought development and amusement park.

Frosty Martin was stirred into a flurry of complicated oil and political development. It began when the Republicans were forced to get rid of Democratic Congressman Byron N. Scott. He was a school teacher with socialist leanings, which led him into an association with Earl Browder, the Communist presidential candidate. In 1937, Scott attempted to steer through Congress, legislation which put at risk the title deeds to a great many California properties.

California was then a Democratic stronghold and only Mayor Thomas M. Eaton was a strong enough Republican, to knock him out

By the late 1940's and early 50's Frosty was a power to reckon with in Southern California.

in the 1938 congressional elections. However, he didn't have the $2,000 needed to gain the nominations. This obstacle was overcome, when Frosty put up $1,000 and Ward Johnson, a lawyer, put up the other $1,000 conditional on Lawrence A. Collins, a rich electric baby-bottle manufacturer, managing Eaton's campaign.

Eaton won. Collins went to Washington and stayed there nine months organizing his office.

When he returned he found Frosty, Ward Johnson and oil man John W. Alford had bankrolled John W. Hampton to start a weekly throwaway paper, The Long Beach Independent. The first issue was Sept. 1, 1938, and 54,000 copies were thrown away.

Collins found the paper $33,000 in the red and the trio were being called upon for more money. They ousted Hampton and put Collins in to run it as sole general partner. Collins got it into the black only after another $24,000 had been put in.

None of them had ever had any previous newspaper experience. But this didn't spook Frosty. He harked back to the wild days of Turner Valley of 1914, when George E. Buck started a weekly paper to afflict the comfortable and comfort the afflicted. Frosty was determined, however, this would be no fly-by-night effort. This would not remain

Frosty Martin.

a pallid advertising handbill, in which the strongest editorial opinion offered was against dogs running loose. The real purpose of this paper was to goad the harbour commissioners into ladling out its riches, for port development. However, they refused to allow private entrepreneurs to take on the job. They decided to develop it as a publicly financed utility.

Alford thought there was some dirty work afoot. The Independent ran editorial after editorial to keep that issue alive.

The long-established daily was the Press-Telegram and Sun with morning and afternoon editions, an organ of the Democrats and the Establishment. But the citizens were delighted to see civic politics vigorously vented and the Republican cause espoused in a small weekly, which never looked back and later became a daily itself.

The Independent was founded in a day when the economics of the business still made it possible, for a crusading group to put enough money together to start a newspaper on a shoestring. Such an effort today would require $10 million, more likely $25 million. In 1938, it was possible for under $50,000 and respectable to do so.

Less than three months after it hit the streets, The Independent was at war with the harbour commissioners for letting a contract to an oil company. The editor alleged the company was a fly-by-night outfit, which would rob the city of its birthright. Council ordered the commissioners to rescind the contract.

In March, 1939, a "cost plus" contract was signed with a consortium of six operators, the Long Beach Oil Development Company. But once again The Independent trumpeted against this contract, too. However, the council refused to budge this time.

In the June civic election, the voters endorsed the stand of the fighting little paper and turned out the "rascals" in city council, who had voted for the "cost plus" contract. The first act of council was to drop four of the harbour commissioners. Then with its own men in control, the paper made a very curious discovery: the contract signed by the old board turned out to be the most fabulous in the history of the U.S. oil patch.

Irwin M. Stevens, a local laundryman and chairman of the board, in his ignorance of the oil business demanded — and got — 30 per cent of each well's oil until the company had been reimbursed for drilling, after which the city would receive 85.5 per cent. Wow!

No more editorials were written, except the Independent mumbled something in its beard, about making sure the commissioners made the consortium live up to its contract responsibilities.

Frosty had been asked two times previously to serve as a harbour commissioner but declined. After his paper won a great victory, he was now an influential force in the city; he liked the limelight and was not averse to playing the "big shot." He decided it was the only sporting thing to do to accept the third request. He did so at age 66, an age when most men are ready to retire. But he decided to "build the darndest seaport you ever saw." And he did.

He did it on one condition: that the board be allowed to run its affairs "like it was our own business." His bold stand in the face of politics which had plagued the board for many years, won him immediate election as chairman. He served until his death.

In the first dozen years after his appointment, 590 wells were drilled for an investment of $70 million.

His biggest conundrum was how to make a seaport with oil under it, a seaport and an oil producer at the same time. How could ships be brought into a harbour full of oil rigs?

His good luck ring found a way of doing both simultaneously. He found a driller, John Eastman, who had developed a procedure called "whipstocking" wells. In this procedure, a spoon-shaped wedge is dropped into a hole that has been started on dry land. This slants the well away from perpendicular and, depending upon the skill of the driller, the hole can be twisted out under the water right into the oil pool. This meant the rigs could be set along the piers, thus leaving the waters of the harbour free for navigation.

As the result of the drilling, money began flowing into the harbour commission faster than it could be spent. At one point, the wells were producing 60,000 barrels a day, thus making the board one of the biggest independent producers in California. Oil was bringing $3 million a month into city coffers a dozen years after Frosty became chairman. And although $40 million had been spent on new piers, a surplus of $70 million existed.

Although he spent the largest part of his time around the harbour Frosty Martin didn't neglect his other interests.

The same day as he was elected to the harbour commission, Sept. 1, 1939, The Independent began publishing three days a week. Then the company bought the Sunday News-Signal. Collins took over both as editor and fired Ray Miller, the only newspaperman of the bunch.

The outstanding success of the paper has been attributed to two important policies of Martin:

1. He never interfered with editorial policy. When any of his friends at the Petroleum Club complained about Collins' editorial policy, Frosty's stock reply was: "I can't do a goddam thing with that four-eyed son of a bitch, Collins." Period.

2. Despite the fact the paper espoused a Republican slant, the opposition always got a chance to have a say: in a front page editorial column written by a Democrat. This did more than anything to create a balance which the readers liked.

By 1943, its stature had risen to the extent that the publication began appearing six days a week. In 1947 a Sunday edition was added. The Press-Telegram pulled out of the morning field and concentrated on its afternoon edition. Frosty then turned over his shares to Spud and step-son Harold Blythe. They kept it five years and sold to the Herman H. Ridder chain.

In the 14 years it existed, Frosty drew $400,000 in dividends and another $300,000 when he sold the paper.

Congressman Tom Eaton died of cancer in office. In the 1940 elections when Democrat Scott ran again, he treated the Republican campaigners, headed by Ward Johnson, with a press campaign which had helped defeat him in 1938. A new weekly, The Chronicle, was set up by Hampton and Oilman Carl Winter, (who had a bone to pick with the harbour board), and filled it full of libel. But there was better libel in the Long Beach Independent and Johnson won. The Chronicle disappeared in a few weeks.

Later another weekly, the Democrat-financed Tribune, with Ray Miller as editor, tried to prove Frosty was a dictator at the harbour board. This wasn't libel. It was the truth. Being a dictator worked. The Tribune revealed secret meetings of Martin's pals at his mansion in Palm Springs. All that proved, however, was that Frosty had "discovered" the desert resort of Palm Springs before Bob Hope and the rest of the movie stars.

In conducting business the way he did, Frosty's ambition was always to build the most modern harbour in the world. And if, as some accusers alleged, he looked upon Long Beach harbour as his baby, what great institution is not but the lengthened shadow of one man?

Frosty would do a good turn for anyone, but when he was on the prowl for business for the port, he was an adversary to watch closely. In the summer of 1947, when it was made public that California Standard and Texaco had combined to build a 1,000-mile oil pipeline across Saudi Arabia, from the Persian Gulf to the Mediterranean Sea, and the pipe would be fabricated in Consolidated Steel's Maywood plant near Long Beach, Martin went after the business. He made phone call after phone call even though he was suffering a severe illness at the time. The port won the contract.

This proved to be the biggest commercial shipment of pipeline in history. It amounted to 1.5 million tons and kept the port busy for three years. The last shipment was made in June, 1950, and had brought in $500,00 in revenue. The last section of the pipe was painted gold and was accompanied by a scroll addressed to the King of Saudi Arabia.

A year before the onset of the Second World War, the United States Navy decided to build a new naval station and shipyard in California. Frosty Martin was part of the civic team that persuaded the navy it should buy a 49-acre site on Terminal Island in Long Beach harbour. He then went about negotiating a deal with Admiral Ben Moreell, then head of the navy bureau of docks and ships and later the man who went on to spark the Sea Bees, (naval construction battalions so important to landing to landing parties), during the war.

On a cold day in December, 1940, Secretary of the Navy Edison came down to Long Beach to confirm the deal and get things moving.

To get out of the cold sea wind, the two of them stood behind a deserted shack to talk. There and then they concluded a handshake deal. Moreell recounted:

"It did not take us long to reach an agreement. I asked Frosty how much Long Beach wanted for the site and he replied: 'We think the navy should pay Long Beach $1 million and give us the right to continue our oil drilling program by whipstocking the wells and extracting the oil from under the naval base.'

"I replied: 'Frosty, your price is too high. I will split the difference. I will give you $1 for the surface rights and give you the right to drill directionally under our land and pump oil.'

"Frosty replied in a matter-of-fact manner: 'That's fair. It's a deal.' And that was that!"

On Dec. 10, 1940, immediately after the deal was made, the harbour commissioners received a cheque for $1.

This proved to be one of the best mutual agreements ever written between a city and a federal government department, even though from a historical standpoint, the transaction has a marked semblance to the purchase of Manhatten from the Indians for $24 and a string of beads.

The navy expanded the yard to four times its original size. The navy also built a hospital and $125 million worth of other works. Many of these were obtained when Frosty made personal visits to the Pentagon in Washington and knocked on doors.

In Frosty's opinion the military had a certain operational code — 'lie as much as you can and steal as much as you can.' — Frosty believed he had to protect the interests of the port against the military. The harbour commissioners had started construction of a new pier just before the U.S. entered the war in December, 1941. It was not finished by the time the navy had grabbed every man and every I-beam in the port. This meant the commissioners had to shut down their expansion. However, they had a large stockpile of steel on hand to finish the job. Frosty ordered it buried in the sand.

Said he:

"When the government became active around here because of the war effort, we figured there was no use in tempting it with a stockpile of steel. To ensure it would still be there when peace came, we buried it well and truly under the sand. Then we were able to proceed with our expansion when the appropriate time came after the war." Frosty quickly learned the business of running a port:

"If you want to stay in this business, you've got to keep your guard up all the time. If you don't, someone will slip in on you and poke you in the nose before you know it."

Early in his tenure of office, Martin laid down the dictum that the board would be a policy-forming body only — period. Operation of the department must be entirely up to the staff. And if they didn't deliver they knew they would be replaced. However, Martin knew in detail everything that was going on. He could be found somewhere around the harbour area almost any day — or night — watching the mushrooming growth. Beginning with 9½ acres above water it grew to several thousand.

He could be salty tongued when he had to. Charles Vickers, the port authority manager in 1964, tells the story of a bidder on a project who wanted a chance to submit a new bid after close of tenders. He became abusive when he was told this wasn't the way business was done by the harbour commissioners and threatened to sue.

"Do you ever play poker?" Frosty asked.

"Yes," replied the contractor.

"How many times do you play your hand."

"Once."

"Then," replied Martin, "screw you. Go ahead and sue."

This reply promptly chastened the contractor.

Turning hundreds of sailors loose, when their ships came into the port, with nothing to do but drink in fairly seedy bars, was one way of having the town torn to pieces on a fairly regularly basis. The answer was to give them something else to do in the way of recreation. The result was the development of a high-class amusement park and gardens just off the beach.

Thousands of tourists were attracted to this park from all over the world.

The centrepiece today — but this did not come in Frosty's time — is the British liner, Queen Mary, which was bought from Cunard on her retirement from trans-Atlantic service, by the harbour commissioners.

When the state and federal governments saw how much money Long Beach was making from oil royalties, they attempted to muscle in on the oil bonanza. The issue was not settled during Frosty's lifetime, but during the 10 years it was going through the courts the fund was put in escrow. The court ruled in favour of the State of California, which managed to pick off most of the jackpot. However, there was enough left — about $80 million — to buy the Queen Mary and bring her to Long Beach harbour and give her a permanent home. It was refitted as a tourist attraction. In this respect, it has been a crowning and imaginative project which would have delighted Frosty.

Another tourist attraction for a long time has been the "Spruce Goose." This was a creation of the eccentric milllionaire, Howard Hughes, whose Hughes Aircraft Company, was located in southern

California. Frosty negotiated with him to have his huge experimental flying boat built for the U.S. Defence Department constructed and assembled in a Long Beach drydock in the harbour, in 1947.

Although it was officially named Hercules, it soon took on the name "Spruce Goose," because of its wood and plywood construction. Even with this lightweight construction, it weighed 200 tons. It is 219 feet long, has a 320-foot wingspread and the rudder towers 80 feet above the keel. There are eight engines providing 24,000 horsepower. Fuel capacity is 14,000 gallons. It was designed to carry 120,000 pounds of cargo and 750 soldiers.

Up to $25 million was spent on the project before it was cancelled. But Hughes spent several million of his own money in order to complete it and made several test flights in Long Beach harbour. Then it was put in a sheet aluminum hangar in the harbour where it still exists.

Man's knowledge of the use of plywood was increased during this historic project. Much of the other know-how was used when President Lyndon B. Johnson ordered a giant troop-carrying plane in late 1964. And, of course, the Russians have one, too.

W.R. Martin.

Chapter 25

Frosty Martin
the Inventor

*F*rosty Martin was the man who first came up with the idea for guiding ships into port by radar, when foggy weather — which was often — halted navigation into Long Beach. Spud gave him the idea as the result of seeing radar work so well in aircraft where it was introduced during the Second World War in the port of Liverpool, England.

Spud had had extensive experience with the ground control approach system for aircraft, in which the pilot of an approaching aircraft is "talked down" to within 50 feet of the centre of the runway. He saw no reason why a shore-based radar control station operator could not contact an incoming ship after the port pilot had boarded it. The port pilot would carry a walkie-talkie which kept him in contact with the radar operator.

Sperry Gyroscope Company made an experimental installation of the radar in March, 1949, at the southern most tip of Pier A in the outer harbour. (At the time this was claimed to be the longest pier in the world, covering 200 acres in area, with a $1.7 million warehouse without a single roof-supporting pillar.) A radar scanner was mounted atop a converted 122-foot steel oil derrick, alongside the port pilot station. The scanner was hooked to a 12-inch radar screen in the station.

The procedure worked the way Spud suggested. During a fog the scanner could pick up the position of ships from as far distant as 30 miles. It was thus possible for the radar man to guide the pilot boat to the ship, which could not be seen until within a few feet of it. After the pilot reached the ship, carrying a walkie-talkie on his back, he contacted the port radar man. The radar operator, after determining the course the pilot should follow to clear the breakwater, other ships at anchor and channel buoys, then gave the pilot data for manoeuvring the ship into a position down the entrance fairway, tracked it in range and bearing and guided it into the harbour and the proper berth.

This system was valuable even for ships which carried their own radar, but were not sufficiently familiar with the port's topography to rely on a "blind approach." Commercial radar was also used in the reverse movement of ships out of the harbour.

The installation cost $11,350.

"Fog was the nemesis of the shipping industry until the advent of port radar," said Frosty. "Shippers used to lose thousands of dollars a year as the result of ships being tied up outside ports. The time an incoming cargo ship spent anchored outside the Long Beach breakwater used to cost the owners more than $125 an hour in operation costs and stevedoring standby time. Ships could be tied up anywhere from 2 to 48 hours. Anything we could do to reduce these costs brought us more business and, of course, more revenue."

The clincher in the harbour board decision to make a permanent installation of the port radar was Sept. 18, 1949, when 18 ships were guided in and out of port.

Spud, his mother Maude Martin and Frosty.

Frosty told the story of a particularly dense fog, one December day in which a Danish steamer was brought into its berth.

"The dock wallopers didn't even know the ship had berthed until they felt the heaving lines thrown from the ship curling around their feet," he said. "That was a real pea-souper."

In its Jan. 12, 1952, edition the Saturday Evening Post brought Frosty Martin international recognition, for his "darndest seaport" with a cover story by Frank J. Taylor. The story was entitled "The Town With Too Much Money." The title brought an unexpected reaction. Frosty began receiving letters of solicitation from people who assumed the money belonged to him personally and that he could give it away.

A farmer from Alberta, who had once known Frosty, wrote and asked for $25,000 to finance a new farm and machinery. He'd never tell a soul where the money came from.

He received requests from people wanting him to pay off church mortgages, open dentistry offices, keep sons in college so they wouldn't be drafted, wildfire schemes like opening a machine gun factory and an outboard motor factory and to put a bubbling system in lakes to keep the fish alive.

Four Dutchmen from Powell River, B.C. wrote for "some money," adding:

"We are four immigrants and we read in the magazine your town has too much money. We are half a year in Canada and are still poor. Therefore, we cannot start our own business as farmers. It is fun to ask for some money. There is a chance if you have too much money you will give us some."

Another man wrote on a printed letterhead and signed his name at the bottom of his request for some money. He began the missive:

"I know this is an anonymous letter, but . . ."

After he saw some of the group pictures in the story, a man from Oklahoma immediately phoned Frosty. He thought he recognized a man who had run away with his daughter. That was one problem that remained in the "unfinished business" file for a long time.

Although they were not exactly earmarked as tourist attractions, two features of Long Beach harbour created a great deal of attention from tourists.

One was the subsidence of the land around the port which began in 1940 and was thought to be the result of pumping oil from under the harbour. At one time subsidence saw the navy drydock and other installations sink 20 feet.

The problem became so alarming the navy mothballed its shipyard for nearly a year. The problem appeared to have been solved satisfactorily when salt water was run into pumped-out oil wells.

The other was a federal government breakwater 12 miles in length. Frosty had a hand in it and it was completed in 1946, at a cost of $7.5 million. It affords protection against ocean surge to not only Long Beach but neighboring harbours and beaches as well.

In 1945, Frosty had so many irons in the fire he elected to retire from Martin-Decker and sold his interests to Elmer Decker. His flair and ability had made them both rich. He also used psychology. This latter trait was often seen when sending out form letters. He would ask the stenographer to make an error or two in each. He would then correct the error with pen and ink, showing the receiver he, the president, had personally written and read each copy.

The subject of so many entries in Tiny Phillips' scribbler was indeed a man who pursued a broad vision. He always thought big and fought big. There was nothing petty about him.

Frosty Martin grew up at a time in history, when it was possible to achieve the American dream. This was a time, when one could go forth from an oil driller's shack in Pennsylvania and become chairman of a board of harbour commissioners, charged with spending millions of dollars "to make things better for the people."

Frosty even became a member of the board of directors for the Peoples Bank of Lakewood, which he helped organize in 1942. The U.S. banking system allows private citizens to form a company and start a bank. In Canada, where the chartered banking system is in force, it is more difficult for this to happen.

The capital structure of the People's Bank was $100,000 and a surplus of $25,000 when it went into business. At the first board of directors meeting, Frosty was there along with a judge, a rancher, a subdivider, a construction man, a real estate broker and a manufacturer's agent.

By 1954, the bank had expanded from a two-room office in which it started, to three branches. The directors were able to place a sign in the window: "16 Million on Deposit." This took Frosty back more than 30 years previously, to Suffield, where he had been amazed when the Bank of Montreal, one of Canada's chartered banks with branches across Canada, had opened a branch in a wooden shack and hung a sign in the window: "Assets: $14 Million." He had come a long way.

Frosty Martin was an experimenter and an inventor. Many of his innovations have become standard in 21st century life. One such is the house trailer. Another is the co-op apartment or condominium.

Trailer living came in with the advent of high-powered motor cars.

The early trailers were equipped usually with a bed and a stove. Frosty showed the people of Long Beach and Palm Springs, the full potential use of the house trailer in the early '30s.

He designed and built a trailer 24 feet long, 6 feet 4 inches wide and 6 feet 2 inches inside height. It had a drawing room 11 feet long, enough to accomodate six persons with sleeping facilities. Two upper berths folded into the ceiling. A double bed opened out from a davenport and two easy chairs could be folded out if needed.

In the trailer was a telephone, which connected with the driver of the car. He pulled the trailer with an old four-passenger Lincoln coupe. He added a special reserve gas tank of 50 gallons.

The dining room was provided with the latest in luxuries — he called it his "land-going yacht" — gas heater, electric fans, screens, electric and gas lights, running water, clothes closets, a radio, and most important of all, a bar.

The other half was a kitchen in which was a refrigerator, gas stove, sink and equipment for garbage disposal. It was finished in white enamel.

The whole thing cost him $3,200, a pretty fancy price in the days before the value of money really started to go down. Weighing three tons, it had a frame of spruce and steel and was equipped with hydraulic jacks, air brakes, carried water and specially built gas tanks and ventilation system designed by Martin.

On the oceanfront in Long Beach used to sit a large striking-looking pink-painted apartment building. This was the city's first co-op apartment. This revolutionary type of cliff dwelling made it possible for a person to own, rather than merely rent, a suite in an apartment building. To achieve ownership required an entirely new form of legal agreement and the owner had to agree to accept the demands made, by co-operating with his neighbors.

Martin, early in the 1950s, saw the possibilities and potentialities of this type of living as cities grew larger and expansion began to encroach on good agricultural land. He saw the cities would have to build up instead of out. The co-op apartment was a way of getting around the resistance of people who would live in an apartment if they could get away from the vagaries of renting.

He had much difficulty selling his idea. The first time around he couldn't raise enough capital. Later he did raise the required money, but a period of several years had elapsed from when he first started. City commissioners refused to allow him to go ahead at that time, as building costs had skyrocketed and they figured he was under-capitalized.

Not deterred, he reorganized and acquired the necessary capital and construction got under way. However, by the time the startling new apartment was finally built, he was dead.

"He never did get to live in that penthouse which he counted upon so much," said Spud Martin. "He had talked about living up there with an ocean view, for a long time. When it came to new ideas and new concepts, he was irrepressible."

Chapter 26

Tiny Phillips Wildcats at Slave Lake

Although Frosty Martin left Medicine Hat and returned to the United States to fame and fortune, Tiny Phillips chose to remain in his adopted country of Canada, where he carved a niche for himself as a back-up consultant in the oil patch. He moved to Calgary in 1927 and set up a workshop in his basement. He worked out of there as a driller, a top-rated well fisher and, for many years, as a specialist servicing Martin-Decker technical instruments. He was in the field until well after "normal" retirement age. He had invented many types of fishing tools.

One of the last times he was out on a job he drove 500 miles to do a repair on a Martin-Decker weight indicator. He talked to it for a while, gave it a few taps, tightened up some screws — and it made up its mind to work. Then he had a fine visit with the crew on the rig and went home.

He was well liked by everyone and made few enemies. However, he had a manner which made a toolpusher step when he said the word.

He was always in funds and usually had a money-making enterprise operating from the basement, which provided him with enough to visit the Calgary Elks Club, where he spent many times yarning with old-time drillers. By virtue of his membership in the Findlay club, he had a life membership in Calgary.

The cottage enterprise that made him the most money was producing gravel protectors, for car and truck headlights.

The last adventure he noted down in the well-thumbed scribbler began in 1925. He arrived home one Saturday, in Medicine Hat, to find a letter from Frank Poss, an oil company promoter from New York City. Inside was a cheque for $500.

A.P. Phillips (crouched) repairing Martin & Decker weight indicator at Turner Valley, others unidentified.

Poss had been told by a friend in the National Supply Company, that Tiny was the best driller in Alberta to retain, to drill some wildcat wells on a lease he held on Lesser Slave Lake. The letter asked Tiny to make a trip to the area, to see if he could arrange to hire teams to haul a drill rig to the location.

Tiny was only too ready to take the cheque and embark on one more pioneering trip to northern Alberta. This project was to last on and off three years. Despite the fact he was busy at many things, it was largely the challenge of pioneering in a new oil field that took him to the lake, which is 70 miles long and whose eastern tip is 180 miles northwest of Edmonton, but couild only be reached then by the Northern Alberta Railways. Poss's lease was located near Slave Lake, a small Indian town where the Snake River runs into the lake. He thus reached the town with one store and one hotel that fall, by NAR passenger train.

He made a survey trip to the lease and gave Poss an estimate of costs.

About a month later, Poss wrote and told him to draw money deposited to his account in the bank and come to Montreal to meet him.

Tiny arrived in Montreal and met Poss at the Windsor Hotel. He noted in his scribbler:

*Albert Parker (Tiny) Phillips.
Photo: Lanes Studio, Calgary,
Alberta, circa 1900.*

"The minute I saw him I knew he was from New York — and no place else — because of his dress."

Poss's problem was that he hadn't raised enough money to go ahead with drilling. He had paid $30,000 for a 34,000-acre lease after an encouraging report by Trevor W. Starkey, a geologist who worked out of London, England, and Vancouver. He had organized International Oils Inc. to exploit the lease. However, a condition stipulated that unless he spent another $30,000 to exploit the lease, the lease would lapse. He wanted Tiny to help him approach Interior Minister Charles Stewart and ask if he could make a deal, to spend the $30,000 on development of only a portion of the lease or, in the alternative, drop the whole acreage. Federal government work commitments on oil leases in those days were tough.

Obtaining an appointment with a cabinet minister was also tough. It sometimes took a week or two and Poss didn't want to spend that amount of time waiting. Tiny didn't either but they took off for Ottawa anyway.

Later that day they went over to the government buildings to see about an appointment. They sat down and waited. The clerk told them the minister was a busy man but said he would try to obtain an appointment. While we were sitting there a man came into the office and took a look at them and said:

"Howdo, Phillips,"

"I was surprised to see this gentleman," said Tiny. "He was one of the inspectors who inspected the shells made at the plant we ran in Medicine Hat during the First World War. I hadn't seen him for a few years, but he recognized me and we had a short visit recalling old times.

"He asked me what I was after, so I introduced my friend and told him we were there to see the minister. He said OK, he would see what he could do. He went into the minister's office and came out in about a minute and said: 'Just go in he will be pleased to see you."

Poss told the minister his troubles. After hearing the petition and thinking the matter over for a few minutes the minister said:

"How long would it take you to get a drilling outfit up there?"

Tiny replied: "I could have an outfit up there in 30 days."

The minister said: "It's development that's needed in that country." He indicated he would waive some of the regulations if Poss would spend the $30,000 right away drilling the property.

Elated at having saved that amount of money, Poss and Tiny set off for Toledo and bought a string of tools from the National Supply Company. They shipped the outfit north and were ready to spud in by February, 1926.

As there was no road to the eastern end of the lake at that time, the outfit was moved across the lake on the ice. The site was a mile from the lake and it was thus necessary to build a road to the site and haul the equipment overland.

Fred Phillips went up to the lake for three summers on his holidays. His job was to haul supplies from the Village of Slave Lake, to the camp by motorboat.

There was no way of hauling pipe to the drill site by land. There was only a pack trail along which the trees were cut off about a foot above the ground, thus precluding the use of wagons. But there was an armada of small boats and they were used to haul everything, including drill pipe to the site by towing it on rafts.

The camp was set up in the middle of the bush and the only persons around were forest rangers.

Setting up the rig and getting it going was slow work at first because supplies and tools weren't too readily available.

The partners of Poss in International Oils were two New York friends, one of whom had supposedly invented the frosting for electric light bulbs, and the other a building contractor.

One day during the summer of 1927, Tiny received word from Poss that he was going to bring a party of his business friends to

Lesser Slave Lake for the big game hunting season. He asked Tiny to build a nice shack for the hunters. Tiny bought lumber, had it hauled in and built a hunting lodge 24 feet square, with six cots and a round table for playing cards. Later the shack was used to accomodate their womenfolk for summer holidays.

Tiny made the lodge comfortable and had two women cooks on hand. At the drill rig he even built them a bathroom next to the boiler house, by running a hot water pipe from the boiler to the shack and constructing a makeshift shower. As there was always plenty of hot water on tap, they told him it beat the showers they had in their own homes.

The hunting party arrived in Calgary one fine autumn day. Included was Frank Craig, a hot shot industrialist from Detroit. Tiny noted in the scribbler: "He likes to have things his own way. Herding this party around was one of the experiences I never forgot."

Craig gave him the most trouble at first. He always wanted to do things different; usually took his time about things and was invariably late — but got what he wanted in the end. He was the type who raised cain with the tradesmen and demanded the best in service everywhere he went. He, of course, had the money to back up his demands. It wasn't until the party reached the north country with its leavening influence on the so-called amenities of civilization, that he discovered Craig could be "one of the boys." The story of the trip is recorded in the scribbler:

"Poss told me to reserve six sections on a CPR sleeper to Edmonton from Calgary. I made the reservations in the morning and later went to the hotel and met the party.

"Craig wasn't satisfied to stay in Calgary all day.

"What is the use of killing time here? This is just a cow town. Let's go to Edmonton where men are men," Craig said.

"Although I explained I had sleeping car tickets for that night, Craig ordered me to take them back to the CPR and trade them for space on the chair car on the afternoon train to Edmonton. We took off for the Macdonald Hotel in Edmonton.

"When we arrived in Edmonton, all got settled in their rooms but Craig. He stopped to talk to some fellow in the lobby. The rest went up and left him and later I went down to see what had happened. I found him arguing with a bellboy at the door of his room, which was next to the elevator. The room was too noisey for him.

"I tried to smooth things over and said there had been a mistake and called the manager. The manager gave him a suite at the end of the wing. This suited him fine and he called in the other fellows, to show them what a real room was.

"We then spent a day in Edmonton waiting for the twice-weekly Northern Alberta Railways train to Slave Lake. I saw that they were well outfitted with guns and a plentiful supply of liquor and first aid supplies.

"When I came to reserve six sections on the NAR sleeping car, Craig asked what time they would arrive in Slave Lake. I told him it would be 12:30 A.M.

"It was about two miles from the station to the town and there was snow on the ground.

"Craig said nobody was going to put him off at a dark station, in the middle of the night and he informed me that nobody had to get off any train in the woods. He told me to go tell the superintendent of the NAR, to set a sleeper off on the siding for them. The superintendent said that could not be done as the NAR only had one sleeper on the road then.

"Craig said that the CPR had plenty of sleepers and he wanted one of them. I knew the CPR superintendents (the NAR was a joint CPR-CNR operation), so I went up to see him and asked if he would meet Craig. Craig went up to his office and blarneyed him.

"You aren't going to throw us off the train in a snow bank are you?" Craig asked. The superintendent said he was afraid they might

Tiny and Zulah Phillips at their Calgary home, circa 1959.

have to. Craig told him he wanted a sleeping car and would pay for it. After quite a visit, the superintendent told him he could have his private car and chef to look after the party, and that it would be on the end of the train the next day.

"The next day we loaded everything we had in the private car and it was set off at Slave Lake and everybody was happy.

"After breakfast Craig began enquiring about the bus. I told him it would be along pretty soon.

"I had arranged for an old-time teamster to take them to camp. He was a real good religious man, who had freighted in the North when it was nothing but trails and big timber. He came down with his team and wagon to pick up the party.

Frank climbed aboard the wagon and from then on became one of us. He turned out to be a great fellow, always ready to get into anything anyone started, especially a game of cards with the fellows at camp.

I took him out hunting one day a short way from camp and he wanted to bag a deer. I had been out previously and tracked a deer over near a big slough. We went over there and sat on a big log for about 30 minutes.

I heard a noise and I looked up and there was a large buck coming out of the bush, around the slough. I gave Craig the rifle and told him to take his time and take good aim. The deer didn't see us for the bush and walked toward us.

Craig got the gun up and pulled the trigger and, to my surprise, he shot the deer. He had a great story to tell about his hunting prowess.

When the provincial government took over the mineral rights from the federal government, it put the former Poss lease in one of eight areas known as the Allen Reserves. They were held back from exploitation for 30 years, to assure that a long-term financial return would be available.

When that day came in 1964 and drilling finally went ahead there again, there was plenty of excitement caused by the big oil play. There was oil under the Poss lease, but Tiny's cable tools had not been able to reach down deep enough for it.

Tiny did not ever come to know this, for that year he died, at the age of 91.

Albert Parker Phillips (1873-1964)

JOHN T. SCHMIDT

John T. Schmidt was born at Ayr, Ontario in 1923. His early ambition was to be a farmer or a printer. He compromised by becoming an amateur historian and a farm writer, launching a controversial and freewheeling column style at age 15.

During most of his newspaper career, John Schmidt has been a columnist, first with the *Ayr News*, bought by his father, John A., in 1913, and still an independent weekly run by the Schmidt family. In 1949, he went to the Kitchener-Waterloo *Record* as a farm writer. In 1958, he was hired by *The Calgary Herald*, and for 28 years turned out a five-day-a-week agricultural column, without missing a deadline. His byline continues to appear in *Alberta Farm and Ranch Report* and in 12 Southern Alberta weeklies.

Photo: Browarny Photographics Ltd., Calgary, Alberta.

A larger than life character in the truest sense, Schmidt's trademark is in speaking his mind fully and sincerely. Never dull, he always keeps his audiences wondering just what to expect from a writer known to have punctured his share of sacred cows.

John Schmidt lives at Chancellor, Alberta, because nobody knows where it is. His interests include classical music, travelling with wife, Margaret, going to press (occasionally) with his independent publication *The Coyote Call*, and his dog Moses, formerly an American Express credit card holder.

PUBLISHER'S NOTE

Canadiana seekers and historical researchers with a particular interest in prospecting, agriculture and/or pioneer expeditions will enjoy reading the following:

E. Cora Hind by Carlotta Hacker, Fitzhenry & Whiteside Limited, 1979.

William Saunders and His Five Sons: The Story of the Marquis Wheat Family by Elsie M. Pomeroy, Ryerson Press, 1956.

Kate Rice, Prospector by Helen Duncan, Simon & Pierre, 1984.

The Little Giant, George Dawson by Joyce Barkhouse, Natural Heritage, 1989.

Not for Gold Alone — Memoirs of a Prospector, by Franc R. Joubin & D. McCormack Smyth, Deljay Publications, 1989.

Mountain Men by Jacques Hamilton, Calgary Power Ltd., 1975.